THE LAST PRIEST OF HORUS

NCQ TITLES

Legal Fictions
Politics & Letters
On Yeats: Upon a House
Drama & Democracy
Locating Theology

Time Pieces
Critical Paranoia
On Joyce: 3 easy essays
On Eliot
Literary Conversions

Film-texts

A Trip to Rome
A Short Break in Budapest
Magic in Prague
WWW: the weekend that warped the world

A Week in Venice
Four Days in Athens
The Last Priest of Horus

Play-texts

Darwin: an evolutionary entertainment
Strange Meetings & Shorts

Eliotics

In preparation

Rubbishing Hockney & other reviews
On Collecting Walter Benjamin
Autobiography & Class Consciousness
Considering Canterbury Cathedral

*Though each can be read independently,
these NCQ publications, taken together,
comprise a single hyper-text collection.*

THE LAST PRIEST
OF HORUS

a film-text

Bernard Sharratt

New Crisis Quarterly
2015

NEW CRISIS QUARTERLY

ncq@newcrisisquarterly.myzen.co.uk

First published 2015

ISBN : 978-1-910956-18-2

In memory of
Dave Hutton

This film-text was not written with actual film production in mind. In fact, it was originally conceived for the stage, one of a trilogy of plays, intended for the National Theatre in London, one for each auditorium. This was envisaged as playing in the Olivier, with its classical open stage and useful drum revolve, alongside *Darwin* in the traditional proscenium-arch Lyttelton, and *Strange Meetings* in the flexible Cottesloe studio space. Needless to say, the National Theatre, after some consideration, wisely declined this opportunity. It has therefore seemed preferable, now, to present it simply as a continuous film-script, and though it plays with a variety of media genres, it is still primarily intended to be read—and imagined.

Fourth century C. E. Egypt is an appropriate time and setting for my characters and my themes, and the text can easily be supplemented with on-line images of the specified sites along the Nile. Little knowledge of early Christian Egypt is assumed, but some at least of the events and characters are not only imagined. The piece was written in the shadow of the occupation of Iraq.

This film-text could also be read as an 'Egypt' film within what later became a series of NCQ 'city' film-texts, variously set in contemporary Athens, Budapest, Prague, Rome, and Venice, with others perhaps still to come.

A film-text is a particularly suitable form for the 'New Crisis Quarterly' imprint, since that name revives the title of an extremely short-lived periodical, whose first, only, and final issue originally appeared in 1984, under the guise of my *The Literary Labyrinth*. Its editorial programme was to publish reviews of imagined books I didn't feel that I had the time actually to write, so its readers were cheerfully invited, if so inclined, to write those works themselves. In the same spirit, reading a film-text means that most of the work of imagining the film can be done by you, which is part of the fun of writing them.

B.S.
May Day
2015

1. EXTERIOR. EGYPT. TEMPLE WALL.
CLOSE-UP. BRIGHT SUNLIGHT.

Sound FX: regular thud and tap of a mallet & chisel.

Lingering close-up pan across superbly carved and vividly coloured images: frescoes on an Egyptian temple wall. Includes image of the hawk god Horus.

Then white fills the frame:

End Sound FX.

[CREDITS OVER :]

2. EXT. RIVER NILE. DAWN SUNLIGHT.

Dissolve from white to aerial tracking shot of the river Nile in bright dawn sunlight.

A felucca type boat is heading north, using the powerful current and some sail.

Four figures on boat. Rest of Nile empty.

Sequence of high tracking shots of the boat. Follow boat slowly with dissolves & slow changes in the light as the morning advances.

More boats on the river now.

Close in on boat until figures resolved into: two Egyptian priests, MEKHEN aged 70, RAMIR aged 30, and two male servants, AMON aged 60, KADOR aged 30. Kador is steering.

[AS CREDITS END:]

Written:]

> XIII MECHIR,
> CONSULATE OF ARBETION & LULLIANUS,
> REIGN OF EMPEROR CONSTANTIUS II

Boat reaches a quayside. A busy port with large warehouses. In background (CGI) huge grain-ships.

Written:] ALEXANDRIA

The boat passengers begin to disembark.

Written:]

> FEBRUARY 8TH,
> 356 CHRISTIAN ERA.

3. EXT. ALEXANDRIA. QUAYSIDE. MORNING.

Kador and Amon unload light baggage. Ramir helps Mekhen from boat onto quayside. Mekhen is blind.

> MEKHEN *(to Ramir)*
> Amon will show you the way.
> If he remembers.

> AMON
> Of course I remember, High Priest.
> The city may have grown but they
> won't have moved the Prefect's palace.

They begin to move through the busy quayside.

OFFICER *(hostile]*
State your business in Alexandria.

RAMIR
To see the Imperial Prefect, and the
High Priest of All Egypt. Official business.

OFFICER
Whose 'official business'?

MEKHEN
I am Mekhen, High Priest
of the Temple of Horus at Kom Ombo.
My seal of office.

Officer examines seal.

OFFICER
Proceed. Under escort.
To the Imperial Guard.

RAMIR
Are you arresting the High Priest
of the Temple of Horus?!

OFFICER
Not arresting. A precaution.
You can explain your business
to the Commander-General.

All four are marched off.

4. INT. PREFECTURE. MORNING.

Two men are walking and talking together:

*Imperial Prefect MAXIMUS is a tough Roman
politician with precarious executive power in Egypt.
Energetic. Ambitious. Experienced.*

*GEORGE / GEORGOS (hard g sounds) is a
Cappadocian, a businessman. Ambitious. Cynical.*

>   MAXIMUS
> The Emperor wants Athanasius out of the
> way. An end to these sectarian splits and
> faction fights. Athanasius won't compromise.
> You will. You'd better.

>   GEORGOS
> So then what happens to Athanasius?
> You've exiled him twice already.
> He just bounces back.

>   MAXIMUS
> This time we call it treason.
> I can make it stick. There's enough half-arsed
> sabotage, dock-strikes, insurgency lunatics.
> They're all his supporters. So he gets it.
> In the neck.

>   GEORGOS
> Literally? Well, I can certainly proclaim
> some reasonable, sensible compromise.
> The Lord Jesus isn't God *and* man—
> just God-*like* and man.
> We can all live with *a* 'Son of God''.

MAXIMUS
That'll do fine.

GEORGOS
But I can't guarantee any compromise
will work if you execute Athanasius.
It'll inflame half the city.

MAXIMUS
And the other half will rejoice.
Alright, not an execution.
Resisting arrest will do.
After he's safely dead,
you can call him a martyr if you like.
Make him a saint.

GEORGOS
Maybe. A mistaken saint.
Subtle mind but too intellectual.
Might work.

MAXIMUS
Look, Georgos, I have a dozen
damn religions to worry about
in this lousy country.
If you can't get agreement among your lot,
at least get me a ceasefire.
The city's under martial law from tonight.
He should be dead by then.

5. INT. AUDIENCE CHAMBER OF ROMAN COMMANDER CYRIANUS

Mekhen and Ramir stand before Cyrianus.

CYRIANUS
You've chosen a bad moment, priest.
The Bureau of Religious Affairs will
probably see you. But not the Prefect.
Not today

MEKHEN
Tell him this concerns a threat
not only to our temple. But to him too.

RAMIR
A rebellion against the Emperor himself—

CYRIANUS
We have plenty of that in Alexandria already.
Which temple is it, again?

MEKHEN
Kom Ombo. The southern frontier.

CYRIANUS
You've come a long way for nothing.
(Syrianus looks towards an Aide with query.)
Reports?

AIDE *gives negative shrug.*

RAMIR
It also involves the gold market at Ombo.

CYRIANUS
Ah. *(registers Prefect's entrance.]*
Well, perhaps you should tell
the Prefect after all.

Enter MAXIMUS, busy, brusque, energetic.

Entourage includes AIDE 2 and GEORGE.

              MAXIMUS
Cyrianus, tonight. He's preaching.
At the Basilica of Theonas I want him.
(notices Ramir and Mekhen) Who are these?
Out. We have work to do.

              CYRIANUS
Priests. From the Kom Ombo Temple.

              MAXIMUS
See the Religious Affairs Bureau. Not me.

              CYRIANUS
A matter, so they say, of the resistance.
Also involves the gold market—

              MAXIMUS
Kom Ombo. That's Governor Flavius's region.
(pause)
State your case. You have one minute

              MEKHEN
Your regional governor is conspiring
with the christian bishop of Kom Ombo.
To demolish the temple of Horus and Sobek.

              MAXIMUS
So?

              RAMIR *(quickly, decisively)*
And to put the temple's gold depository
under his direct control.
He also plans to move the camel and slave
markets from Daraw to Kom Ombo.

He will then control the revenues from both.
And he will have the support of the christians.
Especially if he destroys the temple.
To build a christian basilica.

Aide has been whispering to Cyrianus.

                CYRIANUS
Sir, Kom Ombo is mainly Nicean.
And the garrison commander
is a recent Nicean convert.
A dangerous alliance.

                MAXIMUS
Agreed. *(pause. decisive. to Aide-2)*
Summon Governor Flavius to Alexandria.
Write to the Council at Kom Ombo:
those markets stay at Daraw till I say so.
And give these priests an order on my
personal command protecting their Temple.
Cyrianus, we need one of our own
in charge of that southern garrison. Fast.
And we need action here, tonight.
Strike the head, the tail will only twitch.

                CYRIANUS *(to Mekhen)*
The Prefect's edict will be ready for you
tomorrow. Take it to the Council at Kom
Ombo. You'll need a full imperial travel
permit after tonight. Get one now, before you
leave. See to it, centurion.

*Ramir and Mekhen go with a centurion to an
antechamber. They overhear the following as they are
given a travel permit.*

                    MAXIMUS
Cyrianus, I want him destroyed tonight.
Use all necessary force.
Georgos, I want you in place
as soon as Athanasius is arrested.

                    GEORGOS
Patriarch Georgos of Alexandria
—at your service.

                    MAXIMUS
Yes, at *my* service, Patriarch.
And don't forget it.

6. EXT. OUTSIDE PREFECTURE. AFTERNOON.

Kador and Amon have been waiting.

                    RAMIR *(elated)*
Better than we'd hoped.
The Prefect's own edict.
By tomorrow.

                    MEKHEN *(cautious)*
Perhaps. If the Prefect can still
give orders by tomorrow.

                    RAMIR
Why shouldn't he?

                    MEKHEN
Let's wait, shall we. We need to find out
what is going to happen tonight.
Time to see an old friend, I think.
Guide us to the Library, Amon.

7. EXT. STREET. POOR DISTRICT.

Two bored Roman soldiers are looking on
 as a TAX COLLECTOR flogs a SHOPKEEPER
in front of his shop.

                    TAX COLLECTOR
          (in time with the blows]
          You owe. Me. Four. Hundred. Where. Is. It?

Undersized EGYPTIAN 1 turns corner into the street.
Shouts to Tax Collector:

                    EGYPTIAN 1
          Oi, what do you think you're doing?

                    SOLDIER 1
          Collecting taxes. What does it look like!

                    EGYTPIAN 1
          For Rome?

                    SOLDIER 2
          None of your business. Scarper.

                    EGYPTIAN 1
          I'm making it my business.

The Egyptian spits in the eye of the soldier
 and runs away, back around the corner.
Soldier 1 pursues him.

Two other Egyptians are waiting for him.
One knifes the soldier, the other steps round the
corner and fires two arrows, killing first
the second soldier, then the tax collector.

*As they drop, a cess-pit collector's cart promptly
appears from the other end of the short street,
pulled by a fourth Egyptian.*

*Egyptian 2 takes a clay token from the dead tax-
collector's wallet and hands it to the Shopkeeper.*

EGYPTIAN 2

Your receipt.

*The three bodies are piled onto the cart,
under the muck, and it continues round the corner.
A smooth fast operation.*

They depart, to shouts of:

EGYPTIAN 3

Bring out yer muck.
Bring out yer muck.

8. INT. LIBRARY OF ALEXANDRIA. AFTERNOON

The librarian, THEON, *is a mathematician,
A vigorous 40-year old. Dignified, serious.
Theon is seated with young (perhaps ten years old)
daughter* HYPATIA, *who is reading to him.
In Greek. From Aristotle, Physics Book VI.*

*Servant TANIB ushers in Mekhen and Ramir,
Kador and Amon, with their baggage.
Mekhen and Theon embrace.*

THEON
It's good to see you again, Mekhen.

MEKHEN
I wish I could say the same, Theon.
But here are my new eyes.
My colleague, Ramir.
My eyes and my Deputy.

THEON
Welcome, Ramir.

RAMIR
I am honoured, sir. I have read your work.
You make mysteries plain.

THEON
Mere mathematics. No mysteries.
Euclid made it all plain, not me.

MEKHEN
You remember my old servant, Amon.
And this is Kador.

THEON
Yes, indeed. Come, sit. Tell me.
Why have you come to this troubled city?
Away from your peaceful temple.

Tanib serves refreshments during the following.
Hypatia helps.

MEKHEN
Our temple is far from peaceful.
The Christians are trying to destroy it.

THEON
Some of them want to destroy my own temple
too: this great library itself. Barbarians.
Emperor Constantine would never have
condoned this. He should never have turned
the empire christian.

RAMIR
Theon, who is Athanasius?
It seems he too is to be destroyed. Tonight.

THEON
I doubt it. He's a survivor. He's been the
Christian Patriarch here for thirty years.
A tough customer.

MEKHEN
But at the Prefecture today someone else
claimed to be Patriarch. Called Georgos?

THEON
Ah, George the Cappadocian. A hard man.
They say he was once bitten by a scorpion.
It was the scorpion that died.
George is just a businessman on the make.
Made his money supplying boots to the
Roman army.

MEKHEN
So why does he call himself Patriarch?

THEON
He isn't. Yet. But being a bishop on the right
side can be pretty profitable these days.

RAMIR
And which is the right side, Theon?

THEON
Depends on the Emperor.
The Arians were condemned as heretics,
thirty years ago, at Constantine's Council,
the Nicean. Athanasius led the attack on them,
and so was made Patriarch of Alexandria as a
reward. But the present Emperor supports the
Arians against the Niceans, so of course our
loyal Prefect, and George, and anyone else
who wants to cash in, is an Arian Christian
too. For now.

RAMIR
So the Prefect plans to replace Athanasius
with this George the Cappadocian?

THEON
Precisely. It won't make much difference to
us. Both sides would happily burn most
of these books. As well as each other.
Whichever side wins, we old believers
are a dying breed.

MEKHEN
Even my fellow High Priest has been
seduced by these Christians
who want to destroy the temple.

RAMIR
But by tomorrow we will have an order
from the Prefect forbidding them.

THEON

If they're Niceans, they won't listen
to the Prefect. He's an Arian.
The Niceans will only obey Athanasius.

RAMIR

So we must see Athanasius as well?

MEKHEN

No, Ramir. We have to see the High Priest
at the Bureau tomorrow. And get the
Prefect's edict. Then travel back to
Kom Ombo as soon as we can. My old body
is feeling too battered to do any more.

RAMIR

Mekhen, you need rest.
But I would like to see this city.
Can you manage without my eyes
for a few hours?

MEKHEN

Yes, of course. Take Amon with you,
he knows the city well enough.
Theon will see for me.
Perhaps even read to me?

THEON

You remember my little daughter Hypatia?
Well, Mekhen, she's old enough now
to read to us both. I'm sorry you can't see
how much she's grown. Amon, bring them
back to my house. It will be safest if you stay
with me tonight.

*Kador gets nondescript cloaks from their baggage,
and hands one to Ramir.*

Amon takes a fairly distinctive cloak. They leave.

Hypatia starts to read to Mekhen.

9. EXT. DOCKSIDE. DUSK.

*In the shadows of a large warehouse, two figures.
A spark in the darkness.
Then a flame as a length of cotton is lit,
then thrown onto a pile of sacks. The fire takes hold.
Figures leave quickly.*

> FIGURE
> Always enjoyed the smell of roasting corn.

10. EXT. STREET IN ALEXANDRIA. DUSK.

*Ramir, Kador and Amon walking.
Streets are almost empty.*

> AMON
> Where do you want to go, Ramir?
> The Pharos, the Harbour,
> the Caesarion, the Serapion—?

> RAMIR
> Well, I would first like to hear
> this Patriarch Athanasius.
> They said he was preaching tonight.

> AMON
> I rather thought so.

KADOR
Remember Ramir, even if the christians
listen to this Patriarch Athanasius,
I doubt if Governor Flavius will.

*As they come level with a small group of christian
clergy, a noisy and colourful cavalcade passes,
forcing everyone to the sides of the street.*

*At centre of cavalcade is PELAGIA, notorious
actress and courtesan, on a magnificent horse.
She is dressed in jewels, see-through gauze and little
else. Slave boys and girls in erotic attire follow her.*

*The clergy are scandalised, turn away,
cover their eyes, make the sign of the cross.*

*All except one, a large fat cheerful monk, NONNUS,
who stands and watches Pelagia in open admiration.*

*As the cavalcade goes out of sight round a corner
Nonnus laughs at his fellow clergy.
Ramir, Kador and Amon listen:*

NONNUS
Shame on you, my brothers, don't you
appreciate such splendid beauty!

CLERGY ONE
Shame on you, Father. That was Pelagia,
the actress. A harlot, a whore.

NONNUS
And a stunning creature.

CLERGY TWO
A cheap courtesan who sells her beauty
to the highest bidder.

CLERGY THREE
To the lowest dregs of the city.

NONNUS
She's hardly cheap! And would you call
our richest fellow citizens 'dregs'.
Perhaps you're right. Still, if she also
dispenses her favours cheaply to the poor,
that surely is a work of true charity.

CLERGY ONE
Charity! She corrupts and leads into sin.

NONNUS
(Laughing at them) Ah, but she makes her
beauty worth the price they pay her for it.
Think how many hours she spends adorning
herself for her lovers. She wants to delight
them —in case those who love her today
don't come back tomorrow.
But we, my brothers, how little time
we spend preparing ourselves to please
our divine lover, the Almighty himself.
Let Pelagia be a lesson to you! *(Great laugh)*

CLERGY THREE
You'll learn the same lesson as her:
you'll both burn in hell!

NONNUS *(Sees Ramir and Amon)*
See, my lord priest, how we christians
love one another!

CLERGY TWO
Don't think we are all like him.

RAMIR
Indeed I don't. But I am told your
Patriarch Athanasius is a great preacher,
a trained rhetorician, a performer.
And he preaches somewhere tonight?

NONNUS
True, one of our finest orators.
Relishes his words. Yes, tonight,
at the Basilica of Theonas.
Just follow Pelagia the Actress!
I'm sure that's where she's going.
She enjoys his skills as much as
her clients enjoy hers. Sadly, I can enjoy
neither myself this evening.
Blessings upon you.

RAMIR
And on you!

Clergy group departs, arguing.
Ramir and Amon continue in the direction indicated.

KADOR
If you're really going to listen
to christian sermons, I'm certainly not.
I'll find my own way to Theon's later.

Kador leaves them.

                    RAMIR
Where's Kador off to? I didn't think
he knew anyone in Alexandria.

                    AMON
Don't ask. I suspect Pelagia has given him
ideas. It is a port city, after all.

11. EXT. STREET. GETTING DARKER.

*Ramir and Amon turn a corner. Their way is partly
blocked by Roman soldiers lined up along the street.
Soldier in charge (rank of sergeant) SERJANUS
comes across to them.*

                    SERJANUS
There's a curfew in this area.
Back to your homes.

                    AMON
What's happening, soldier?

                    SERJANUS
They don't tell us. And we don't tell you.
Now, off the streets.

                    RAMIR
We have the General's own authority.

*Ramir shows Serjanus the travel permit from the
prefecture. Serjanus reads the pass, with difficulty.*

                    SERJANUS
"Two priests, two servants. Permission to
travel. Carrying imperial orders. Assist as
necessary."

*Serjanus hesitates. Ramir assumes a confidential
and authoritative manner.*

                    RAMIR
          A special assignment.
          From the Imperial Prefect himself.

                    SERJANUS:
          Very good, sir. Then you probably know
          more about this operation than I do, sir.

*Serjanus lets them through.
Ramir and Amon walk warily past the line of troops
into an open square. Troops are visible in various
side streets around the square.
Ramir and Amon are now at a side-entrance
to a large basilica.*

                    AMON
          I'm not sure what you're up to, but this is
          where your Athanasius is preaching.

                    RAMIR
          And it looks like a lot of other people are
          hoping to hear him too. Even the military!

*Ramir enters the basilica by the side-entrance.
Amon follows him, reluctantly.*

12. INT. BASILICA. EVENING.

*The basilica is crowded with men, women,
and some children. Standing not seated.*

*ATHANASIUS is in the pulpit. He wears a
magnificent cope. Aged about 60. Grey hair.*

ATHANASIUS
My children in God.
We may sometimes be persecuted by men.
But we are always loved by God. (AMEN)
We may sometimes be hated by men. (AMEN)
But God our Father so loved us that he sent his
only true Son to die for us. (AMEN)
And we must be willing to die for him. (AMEN)
And for the only true faith: that the Son truly is
God. And that the Son truly is man. (AMEN)
But, my children,
martyrs are not made by men.
Martyrdom is always in the hands of God.
If He wills it, our blood will purify the church
of those who do not truly believe in his Son.
(AMEN)
But until he wills it, it is our task to proclaim
that truth always, in the words of the one true
Creed of the Council of Nicea:

CONGREGATION JOINS IN CREED:

We believe in one God,
the Father, the Almighty,
maker of heaven and earth,
of all that is, seen and unseen.
We believe in one Lord, Jesus Christ,
the only Son of God,
eternally begotten of the Father,
God from God, Light from Light,
true God from true God,
begotten, not made,
of one Being with the Father —

*They continue chanting the Athanasian version
of the Creed.*

*As the recitation continues, the main doors
at far end of the church suddenly burst open.*

*Troops pour in, swords drawn. Troops attack.
Screaming and mayhem. Some slaughter.*

Rapid sequence:

*Athanasius is shouting to be heard.
Clergy drag Athanasius out of the pulpit
and into the sanctuary area.*

*Congregation resists the soldiers,
by sheer numbers protecting Athanasius
who stays in the sanctuary.*

*Clergy drag Athanasius into the shadowed recesses
of the basilica, behind the high altar.*

*Just in front of Ramir a woman is horribly skewered
by a soldier. Close-up of her face.*

*Amon tries to intervene but is wounded in the leg
by a soldier. Ramir desperately fights off the soldier
and then drags Amon clear.*

*Ramir drags wounded Amon to rear of basilica, near
the group of clergy now gathered around Athanasius.*

Struggle continues in the main body of the church.

*Some clergy are trying to persuade Athanasius
to save himself.*

> CLERGY-A
> Get out of those vestments, Father.
> You're too easy to recognise.

> CLERGY-B
> You have a duty to escape.
> Let God decide about martyrdom, not you.

*Athanasius is cool and collected.
Even amused at this.*

> ATHANASIUS
> I'm glad you were listening.

> CLERGY-C
> Father, give me your cope.
> They'll follow me while you escape.

*Clergy-C tears the cope off Athanasius, and puts it on
himself. Clergy-C, with a few others, runs across the
sanctuary very visibly. Towards a narrow stairway
leading up into the basilica dome.
Troops spot him and try to go in pursuit, diverted
from the group around the real Athanasius.*

*Amon is lying near the Athanasius group.
He is now unable to move any further
because of the wound in his leg.*

                AMON
        Ramir, I can't move. Leave me. Get out.

                RAMIR
        (impetuous decision)
        Give me your cloak, then.

*Ramir takes the cloak off Amon.
Ramir goes to the group round Athanasius
and throws Amon's cloak over Athanasius.*

                RAMIR
        (to Clergy, pointing to Amon)
        Look after him.
        (decisively to Athanasius)
        Put this on. Follow me.

*Athanasius hesitates briefly, then nods.
Ramir hustles the cloaked Athanasius
to the side entrance through which
Ramir and Amon had entered.*

*As they leave, Cyrianus enters from the main door,
in command. George also enters, with bodyguards.*

13. EXT. STREET OUTSIDE BASILICA SIDE-
ENTRANCE. DARK.

*Serjanus's soldiers are now a few feet outside,
guarding that entrance.*

*Ramir holds Athanasius close to him,
with Amon's distinctive cloak over him.
Ramir urgently summons Serjanus
and waves the permit.*

> RAMIR *(decisively)*
> Soldier, one of my men is wounded.
> Help him. Jump to it.

*Serjanus recognises Ramir and 'Amon'
and remembers the permit.*

*Serjanus clears a path through the soldiers
and helps Ramir to support the cloaked Athanasius
down the street.*

> RAMIR
> Well done, soldier. I'll inform the general,
> personally. But not a word to anyone.
> The general's whole operation depends on it.
> Now, back to your men.
> I can take it from here.

*Serjanus returns, pleased with himself.
Ramir and Athanasius turn a corner out of sight.*

14. EXT. STREET. DARK.

> RAMIR *(laughing with relief.)*
> I'm told you christians believe in miracles.

> ATHANASIUS
> We do indeed. And in guardian angels.

                    RAMIR
I'm no angel.
I'm a priest of the temple of Horus.

                    ATHANASIUS *(broad smile)*
A first-class miracle, then.

                    RAMIR
Perhaps. Now, do you know the way
to the house of Theon the Mathematician?

15. INT. BASILICA.

Melée continues. Cyrianus is joined by George.

                    CYRIANUS
We have him trapped, in the dome.

                    GEORGOS
The new patriarch, at your service.
Tell me when you need me.

                    CYRIANUS
(to officer) Clear this crowd.
Force a way up those stairs.

*Clergy with 'Athanasius' have bolted the heavy door
at the foot of the narrow winding stair up to the dome.*

*Soldiers start to clear the crowd
and try to force a way up the stairs.*

*A furious Pelagia is highly visible among the crowd.
She is being salaciously manhandled by several
ordinary soldiers. Verging on sexual assault.*

16. EXT. STREET. NIGHT.

Soldiers are imposing a curfew, clearing the streets.

Kador is seen slipping past a patrol.
He clearly knows where he is heading
and is anxious to avoid troops.

17. INT. BASILICA.

Soldiers still trying to force the door.

> CYRIANUS
> Burn the whole place if necessary. But get him.

> GEORGOS
> As the new Patriarch, I think I might object
> if you burned my basilica down
> on my very first day—

> CYRIANUS
> If we don't smoke him out
> you won't be patriarch at all.
> Keep trying. They're only damn priests!

18. INT. THEON'S HOUSE. NIGHT.

Athanasius and Ramir have arrived
and already given an account.

> MEKHEN
> You left Amon behind. Injured? How badly?

> ATHANASIUS
> My people will look after him.

THEON
And who will look after you?

ATHANASIUS
This is the third attempt on my life.
I am learning to look after myself.

RAMIR *(to Theon)*
You could hide him. In the Library?

THEON
That's all the excuse the Arians
would need to burn it down!

ATHANASIUS
I would be grateful to stay here,
just for tonight. Tomorrow I will find
a safe house to disappear into.

THEON
Cyrianus will turn the city upside down
when he realises you've escaped.

ATHANASIUS
I can leave the city for a while, if I have to.
There's always the desert.

Sudden commotion at the door.
Anxiety. Tanib opens the door.
Two clergy help limping Amon to enter.
Mekhen embraces Amon.

CLERGY-D *(to Athanasius)*
We thought he *[Ramir]* had handed you over.
But he *[Amon]* said to come here.

                    THEON
The more the merrier.

                    CLERGY-E *(to Athanasius)*
They think you're still trapped in the dome.

19. EXT. STREET. NIGHT.

Kador furtively enters a house in a poor district.

20. INT. UPSTAIRS ROOM INSIDE POOR HOUSE.

Four men. A woman keeps look-out at the window.
The men are dockers and warehousemen.
One has a sword. The others have knives.
Towards the end of a long discussion.

                    MAN-1
So it'll be martial law for weeks now.
The curfew will be strictly enforced.

                    MAN-2
We can still meet at the docks during the day.
But meeting at night will be more dangerous.

Kador enters the room. Subdued greetings.

                    MAN-3
It's good to see you again, Kador.
But you'd best not stay long. The patrols are out.

                    KADOR
We're going back to Kom Ombo tomorrow.
Sooner than I thought. Once I'm back it will be
even more difficult to get messages through.
That worries me. We can't co-ordinate.

                    MAN-1
We don't need to, yet. Quick raids. Strike fast.
Keep the pot boiling. Stick to the strategy.

                    MAN-4
If the Nubians invade again from the south
it will be different. We can be ready for that.

          WOMAN ON LOOK-OUT *interrupts.*
Patrol in sight.

                    MAN-2
Time to scatter.

                    WOMAN
They're only targetting Nicean houses.

                    MAN-1
We can't risk it. Kador, the back way.

                    MAN-4
Keep in contact.

                    KADOR
When I can.

They all leave silently.
Patrols are hammering on doors nearby.

21. INT. THEON'S HOUSE. THE SMALL HOURS.
VERY QUIET.

Everyone is asleep, exhausted.
Except Ramir and Theon.
They are sitting over wine and talking quietly.
Some papyrus rolls in front of them.

Theon has a stylus and a writing tablet.

                    THEON
I told you, no mysteries.
A trick every builder knows.

He draws a triangle to illustrate
the Pythagoras theorem. Points to it.

                    THEON
Three that side, four that side.
If that side is five, this must be
a right angle corner, here.

                    RAMIR
I see. It's a sequence.
Three threes plus four fours equals five fives.
9 plus 16 makes 25. Perfect.

                    THEON
Yes. But don't presume.
Try four fours plus five fives.

                    RAMIR
16 plus 25. Forty-one.

                    THEON
See. Nowhere near six sixes, 36.

                    RAMIR
So you get a different angle?

                    THEON
Far more interesting.
You get a number you can't divide by any other
whole number: 41. Just like 5 fives plus 6 sixes.

Gives you 61. You can't divide that either.
Or 7 sevens plus 8 eights.

       RAMIR
So there is a pattern? A regularity?

       THEON
Maybe. We're not sure yet.
But if there is, it's always been there.
Even if no-one knew it.

       RAMIR
You said there were no mysteries.
When you think about it, that's a mystery.

       THEON
When you really think about it, it isn't.
How could anything so obvious be a mystery?
It's just that we haven't thought about it enough.

       RAMIR
But if numbers have always been there,
how can I make up a new number?
Some enormously large number
that no-one has ever thought of before.

       THEON
That doesn't mean that you've made it up.
You've only discovered it, put it into words.
Our words. Given it a place in our world,
for the first time.
But it's still been there for ever.

       RAMIR
Where is 'there' ?

THEON.
Enough. If you don't mind,
I'm not going to stay up for ever.
It will be a busy day tomorrow.

RAMIR
(looks at glimmering dawn light)
You mean today.

22. INT. BASILICA. DAWN LIGHT.

Soldiers finally force their way up the stairs.
They drag Clergy-C as 'Athanasius'
In front of Cyrianus and George.

Cyrianus tears the cope off the priest
and realises that it's not Athanasius.
He smashes his fist into priest's face. Blood.

CYRIANUS
Idiots! That's not him.
(throws the blood-stained cope to George.)
Spoils of office, George.

GEORGE
Ah, my first spoils. *(looks at blood)*
Not too spoiled, I hope.

CYRIANUS
Take him away. Work on him.
And search every damn Nicean house in the city.
Now!

Soldiers drag Clergy-C away.

23. INT. THEON HOUSE. MORNING.

*In the background, Hypatia is playing a game
of blocks and numbers with the bandaged Amon.*

*Mekhen, helped by Tanib, is preparing to leave.
Enter Ramir and Theon.*

> MEKHEN
> Ramir, we have to move.
> Amon can no longer guide us.
> And Kador has disappeared, as usual.
> Can you find the way, Ramir?
> First the High Priest. Then the Prefect's letters.

> THEON
> Take Tanib, to guide you.
> Is Athanasius still here, Tanib?

> TANIB
> Yes, sir. The city is being torn apart.
> But very few Roman soldiers ever go near a
> church, so they don't know what he looks like.
> They're just arresting anyone who looks sixty
> and dignified.

> THEON
> Keep them out of trouble if you can, Tanib.

24. EXT. STREET. MORNING.

*Ramir, Mekhen, and Tanib in street. Troops are out in
force, making arrests. Houses are being violently
entered. Ramir's group is stopped. The travel pass is
produced.*

SOLDIER
(reading the pass, more or less)
"Two Priests, two servants. Imperial orders."
Proceed. Keep your heads down.

25. INT. OFFICE OF THE HIGH PRIEST OF ALL
EGYPT, AT THE BUREAU OF RELIGIOUS
AFFAIRS. MID-MORNING.

The High Priest, TIBULLUS, *is a Roman career*
official. His main preoccupation is with
temple finances and taxes.

He is lying on a couch, reading a memo,
 and being pleasured by a female slave.

The entrance of Mekhen and Ramir interrupts this.
He waves the girl aside. She stays in the background.

During the scene two other slave-girls offer
refreshments, which Mehken and Ramir decline.

Tibullus is impatient, resenting the interruption.
He knows Mekhen of old.

MEKHEN *(formally)*
Mekhem, High Priest of the Temple of Horus,
presents his respects —
to the Lord High Priest of All Egypt.
And presents also his deputy, Priest Ramir.

TIBULLUS
I'd rather you presented your temple taxes
on time, Mekhen. I've read your letter.

You pick an interesting moment to complain
about your fellow High Priest, this Nebre.

          MEKHEN
Nebre is no longer a High Priest.
He has gone over to the christians.

          TIBULLUS
It happens. And *(maliciously)*
I see your eyes have finally gone as well.
Now I'll have to replace both Nebre and you?

          MEKHEN
My physical blindness is my misfortune.
Nebre's moral blindness is deliberate.
He intends to turn over the Temple of Sobek
to the christians. They will build a church
on its ruins.

          TIBULLUS
Awkward for you.
Your temple of Horus is next door?

          MEKHEN
It is the same temple, but divided
into two sanctuaries. Sobek and Horus.

          TIBULLUS
Ah, I remember. A unique arrangement.
Expensive. Two courts, two colonnades,
two hypostyles—

          MEKHEN
But the same building.
And all of it is sacred to the gods.

TIBULLUS
Yes, but to the old gods. Our present Emperor
rather favours the newer gods. And as his
religious affairs representative, I merely make
sure that whichever gods the people happen to
fancy, the Emperor isn't out of pocket. Your
doctrinal squabbles are not really my concern.

RAMIR
But if half the temple goes,
half the tax revenue will go too.

TIBULLUS
If the christians build a church there,
I will simply get it from them instead.

RAMIR
And what if the regional governor
gives them tax exemptions?

TIBULLUS
That would be exceeding his powers.

RAMIR
He may try to decide his own powers soon.

TIBULLUS
Meaning?

RAMIR *(decisively)*
Governor Flavius wants to control the supply
routes from the gold mines in the Eastern Desert.
And the camel and spice trade from Nubia.

TIBULLUS
So —

RAMIR

If he also has the Nicean christians on his side
and then offers a deal to the Nubians
across the border, he can soon take over the
entire southern province for himself.

TIBULLUS

Interesting analysis. For a priest.
But not quite the concern of my
Bureau of Religious Affairs.

RAMIR

Not directly. But the Imperial Prefect must
realise that if the Niceans also control
the port of Alexandria, and so the corn supply to
Constantinople, your Arian Emperor may soon
have lost the whole of Egypt, north and south.
And the Empire can't survive without Egyptian
corn. Correct? Hence the order to arrest
Athanasius last night?

TIBULLUS

Indeed. Full marks. Most people think we're just
arguing about the shape of god. The corn supply is
much more important. *(pause)* I think perhaps it's
time the Temple of Sobek had a change of
personnel. You're rather young, Ramir,
to be a High Priest. But perhaps Deputy at the
Temple of Sobek might do for now,
with right of succession if —for example—
High Priest Nebre should decide he'd rather be a
christian bishop instead. Perhaps even in some
independent little kingdom. I assume you'd
be just as happy to serve a crocodile as a hawk.

26. SUDDEN FLASH INSERT. RAPID IMAGES.

Full screen. Almost subliminal:
Crocodile attacking a woman.
Churning water. Blood.
Extreme close-up of woman's face
in terror as she is savaged by crocodile.
(This is Ramir's memory flashback
which should startle and puzzle the audience here]

27. BACK TO INT. HIGH PRIEST OFFICE.
CONTINUOUS.

> RAMIR
> I would be honoured to serve
> any of our ancient gods.

Tibullus takes a writing tablet and stylus
from a slave-girl and starts writing.

> TIBULLUS
> Perhaps you should serve *both* Horus and Sobek.
> You're already Deputy to Mekhen. If I also give
> you right of succession to the Temple of Horus,
> we might soon have a much more economical
> arrangement at Kom Ombo. These days I really
> can't justify the expense of two priesthoods.
> There isn't the demand.

He stops writing, applies his signet ring,
and hands over the tablet to Ramir.

> TIBULLUS
> Your official letters of appointment, Ramir.
> Satisfied, Mehken? Now, I have rather more
> pressing matters to attend to.

28. EXT. OUTSIDE BUREAU.

Tanib has been waiting for them.

>   MEKHEN
> Ramir, are you quite sure your main concern
> is still to save the temple?

>   RAMIR
> Of course. But I'm beginning to think the best
> way to do that may be to save Egypt.

>   MEKHEN
> From what, precisely?

>   RAMIR
> From Roman High Priests. Roman high taxes.
> Roman gods. Roman morals.

>   MEKHEN
> A large agenda.

>   RAMIR
> The christians believe in miracles.

>   MEKHEN
> We're not christians. The Prefecture.
> The edict. Then Theon's.
> Then back to Kom Ombo.
> That's the agenda, Ramir. No miracles.
> Tanib, guide us, please.

29. INT. PREFECTURE. MORNING.

An angry Pelagia confronts the Prefect's Aide.

          PELAGIA
I'll have his balls for this.
How dare he order an assault on a public hall.
I'm not even a christian. I was lucky to escape
with my life. I have friends in high places,
I can tell you. Lots of them. And they can skin
him alive as far as I'm concerned.
He hasn't heard the last of this.

She storms out.

30. INT. THEON'S HOUSE. AFTERNOON.

Mekhen attends to the injured Amon,
with Hypatia's help.

Ramir and Athanasius in quiet conversation.

Kador has returned and is making preparations
for a journey while unobtrusively listening.

          ATHANASIUS
I'm sorry to disappoint you, Ramir.
The Prefect is mistaken. The corn supply to
Constantinople is not at all my concern.

          RAMIR
But you do command the allegiance of many
Nicean christians in Alexandria,
who work in the harbour,
the warehouses, transport?

                    ATHANASIUS
I will command nobody's allegiance if I am
arrested. I will simply be another martyr
for the faith. The true faith.

                    RAMIR
Do you have the right to become a martyr
when your people need you?

                    ATHANASIUS
I am the servant of my Lord God.
I will not seek martyrdom if the good Lord
contrives a few more miracles
to deprive me of it!

                    RAMIR
So you will escape?

                    ATHANASIUS
Cyrianus's troops are watching every true
christian household in Alexandria.
If I can get south to the monasteries of
Anthony or Pachomius I will be safe for a while.

Mekhen is led over by Tanib.

                    MEKHEN
It's time to go, Ramir. We will have to leave
Amon behind. Theon says he will take care
of him until he is well enough to travel.

Ramir takes Mekhen aside to talk.
Brief, urgent. Inaudible.

Then returns to Athanasius.

RAMIR
Patriarch Athanasius, it's time for you
to practise being a servant of a new Lord.
The Lord High Priest of Horus at Kom Ombo.
We still have an imperial permit
for two servants to travel south with us.
And we're short of a servant right now.
Would you like the job?

ATHANASIUS *(smiles)*
The good Lord hasn't lost his touch.

RAMIR
It's time for your cloak again, my lord servant.
(hands him clothes)
And you carry the bags, I'm afraid.

29. EXT. THEON'S HOUSE. AFTERNOON.

Mekhen, Ramir, Kador, and Athanasius,
who is now dressed as a servant, leave.
Theon waves them off, Hypatia at his side.

30. EXT. QUAYSIDE. LATE AFTERNOON.

Ramir, Mekhen, Kador, with Athanasius in servant
clothes and carrying baggage.
The permit clears their departure.
They board the boat on the canal leading to the Nile.
Cast off. Travelling south.

31. INT. PREFECTURE.

MAXIMUS *(to Aide-2)*
I've got enough trouble without that tart Pelagia
sticking her vicious little knife into my back.

                    AIDE-2
She does have a great many powerful clients,
I'm afraid, sir.

Cyrianus enters, with several soldiers.

*Two are more or less dragging Clergy-C, who is now
badly bloodied and beaten up, and is very nearly dead.*

*Two more are holding Clergy-B, only slightly bruised.
Both clergy are blindfolded and bound.*

                    MAXIMUS
Report, Cyrianus.

                    CYRIANUS
Athanasius is probably through the cordon
by now, sir. But we've got two of his priests,
one last night,one just now.
They won't talk. So far.

                    MAXIMUS
(inspects the near-dead Clergy-C.)
Well, we won't get much out of him.
Your men need more practice, Cyrianus.
I want answers, not corpses.
(points to Clergy-B)
Take his blindfold off. *(soldier does so.)*
(to Clergy-B)
Fancy yourself as a martyr, do you?
(points to Clergy-C.) Like that?
(Clergy-B looks at the tortured Clergy-C.)
(pause)
Where is Athanasius?
(Waits. No response.)
Or like this — ?

*(Maximus viciously knifes Clergy-C, who dies.
Still no response from Clergy-B.)*
(wearily) Take them away.
And practise. On him *(Clergy-B.)*
(Soldiers drag away both clergy.]
Right, Cyrianus.
We know where he's gone anyway.
Alert the Nile garrisons. The dragon will be
heading for his desert lairs again.

32. EXT. BOAT ON NILE. NIGHT.

*Fade up to: Crescent moon in clear night sky.
Boat is silently gliding south. Sail is full.*

*Throughout the scene, the boat visibly moves
against the dark strongly flowing current.
Moonlight gleaming on water. Banks dim.*

*This long sequence begins in almost black & white,
but as cinematographically breath-taking as possible.
Frequent close-ups on faces.
Play of light, shadow, reflections.*

*Dawn light, in colour, is glimmering
by the very end of the sequence.*

*Kador steers.
Mekhen is apparently asleep in the bow.*

*A quiet conversation between Ramir and Athanasius
has already lasted for some time.*

Kador is listening but does not intervene, yet.

RAMIR
Niceans. Arians. I don't understand.
It's a difference of one letter, a tiny iota,
and because of that little letter
you christians are slaughtering each other?

ATHANASIUS
A great deal hinges on that one letter.
Whether the Father and the Son are one God.
The *same* substance, or just *similar*.
Hom*o*-ousios or hom*oi*-ousios.

RAMIR
Does your god only speak Greek?

ATHANASIUS
Other languages make the same distinction.
Latin: *Con*-substantialis. *Co*-substantialis

RAMIR
That's not the same distinction.
(smiles) Only similar.
Languages defeat such translations.

ATHANASIUS
Language defeats such thoughts.
Whenever I try to think about God
I feel more and more the inadequacy
of any language.

RAMIR
Yet I'm told it was you who provided that
very language for your fellow believers.
It's your words they recite to express their
faith, their creed?

ATHANASIUS
People need to express what they believe.
We have to do that in language.

RAMIR
But you try to define. One God, many gods.
Three persons in one God. Two natures, one
man. *(pause)* It is better to tell stories.
To show images. Pictures for the mind.
The world is shaped as a story,
not as a definition.

ATHANASIUS
Images can deceive, stories can lie.
Shadows in a cave for those who have
never seen the sun. You've read Plato.

RAMIR
Of course. The parable of the cave.
But Plato thought the truth lay in numbers,
not in images, or even words.

ATHANASIUS
(pause) Look at the moon. A pale sun.
If that was all the light we ever saw
or saw by, how could we know that the world
is not dark and colourless, but we do know
(he gestures round) that the banks are green
with growth, that the Nile itself is blue. We
could not even conceive of the great blazing
sun if all we had ever seen was the pale moon.

RAMIR
But the water is not blue. That is only a
reflection of the sky by day. An image. Look.

*Ramir puts his hand in the water and holds it up
so that drops fall, catching the moonlight.*

                    RAMIR
Neither blue nor dark. Colourless, transparent.
And each drop is fragile,
lasting only a moment as it falls.
But it falls back into this great river,
and all those tiny drops together make a
mighty current that this boat can barely push
against, even with the power of the wind
behind it. *(pause)*
And yet each drop contains life itself.
That is what gives life to those green banks.
Almost invisible drops, yet a powerful,
mighty river. Life-giving. A god. *(pause)*
We cannot see the sunlight itself either,
only the sun that gives us light, shadows,
reflections of the light. But that light also
gives life. A god.

                    ATHANASIUS
Water and sun give life only briefly to our
world. The desert sun demands death.
And flood-waters drown us. We die.
That is the truth of this world.
I want the sun that lasts for ever, the world
beyond this world of mere moonlight.
My god died. And rose again.

                    RAMIR
An old story. Osiris.

                    ATHANASIUS
But my god was truly a man, not just a story,
a god who died not only in an image.

Homo-ousios. The same being. God and man.
My god really died in this world. As I will.
As my people died two days ago on the
swords of the soldiers of Rome. *(long pause)*
When I was a child, the empire was still
pagan. My church was persecuted by the
Emperor, Diocletian. I saw christians ripped
apart by wild beasts, for the entertainment of
a holiday crowd. Nailed to pillars, doused in
tar and set on fire as human torches, to light
up the night in public gardens. Yet they died
singing. *(pause)* My Christ really died and
really conquered death, so we can face even
such deaths and know it is not the end,
but a way to a world beyond death.

    RAMIR
—And now the Emperor himself says he is
a christian. So christians can kill other
christians because they disagree about a word,
a tiny letter?

    ATHANASIUS
About the truth. That is worth dying for.

Kador finally intervenes. Very angry.

    KADOR
And worth killing for? Your christian people
kill each other because you disagree about
the next world. The Romans kill my people
every day in this world. From hunger and
starvation. Those green banks grow enough
corn to feed the whole of Egypt. But the
Romans take it and send it to their capital
city, Constantinople.

They take it to feed the army that forces us
to pay the taxes. What does your Christ say
about that kind of world?

ATHANASIUS
I was born in this country too. The world is
full of such evil. The world belongs to evil,
until Christ comes again. Till then we must
render to Caesar what is Caesar's.
To God what belongs to God.

KADOR
A fine story! You think Egypt belongs to
Caesar?

RAMIR
And our temple belongs to *our* gods,
Athanasius. Yet the christians at Kom Ombo
want to take it for their god. Your god.

KADOR
It's the gold they really want to take,
for themselves. Do you know *why*
there is a temple at Kom Ombo? Because of
the traffic from the gold and silver mines.
People condemned to live their whole lives
in deep caves. Never to see the sun.
That's not a parable of some philosopher.
That's a life sentence.
(pause. Kador is remembering:)
Deep down in the mines, the rocks are blacker
than this night. But the veins of silver are
so brilliantly white that they seemed like
sunlight in the lamps we wore.
And the gold-bearing rock is so hard
we had to soften it with fire.

Naked men, women, and children in the heat
and light of fire, choking in the smoke.
Then hammering at the rock, endlessly.
Reducing it to powder. For a few small grains
of gold. For the wealth we must render to
Caesar. Why should we simply wait for your
Christ to come to end that living death?

Anger is mounting.

Mekhen has been awake for some time, listening.
He now intervenes to calm tensions down.

      MEKHEN
But, Kador, you escaped from those mines.
Came to our temple. You are safe.
You can now enjoy the sun. *(pause)* I looked
at the sun directly, once. During an eclipse.
Now I can no longer see the sun or the moon.
My world is always dark night. No images.
Not even shadows. And I will enter the
kingdom of the dead sooner than any of you.
(pause) But I can still see inside myself.
And that is where the evil of this world comes
from, not from Caesar or from somebody
else's false beliefs. Good men have believed
many different things. So have cruel men.
But Evil itself is from the heart. Until we
weigh the heart on the scales of justice,
we will continue to kill. For gold. For corn.
For power. For this Caesar and that god.
Even for definitions. *(pause)* But for ordinary
people, who do not live by definitions,
who have no power, who till the soil,
who make those fields fertile with corn,
their gods are not just stories or images.

And for them the temple is not Caesar's,
nor simply the house of a god.
For them it is their hospital, their school,
their hope. Their comfort.
They are not concerned with definitions.
But they do need a god in their lives.
Let them keep their old gods.
Do the new gods offer more?
(to Athanasius) Patriarch Athanasius,
will you allow your christians to take away
their temple from my people?

The sun has begun to rise. Magnificently.

ATHANASIUS
High Priest Mekhen, I owe you a miracle.
I promise I will write to the bishop of Kom
Ombo. When we get to the monastery of
Pachomius. *(pause)* We should arrive at the
monastery by tomorrow. Perhaps then you
will see what the new god has to offer.
Even what a new world might be like.
Pachomius left this world and conquered
the desert. He is dead now. But the monastery
he founded has remained a community of
peace and love among brothers. They have
chosen shared poverty, not wealth.
Not gold for themselves, but work for others.
A foretaste of paradise, even on this earth.

*Camera pulls back slowly to show the boat in the
clear light of the rising sun.*

*Blue river, green banks, golden reflections of the sun
in the water.*
Then a close-up focus on reflections in the water.

33. EXT. MONASTERY AT PHBOW.
LATE AFTERNOON.

Phbow is on the east bank of the Nile.
Right at the edge of the river.
The monastery is a collection of roughly built
long houses, each containing twenty cells,
each cell with three monks.
One large building is in the centre.

Monks are working at different activities:
each trade outside specific houses:
mat, basket, and rope weaving from rushes;
metalworking, shoemaking, dyeing;
carpenters, copyists.

Each group of 20 is under a supervisor
but the supervisor works alongside the rest.

The monks are all dressed alike: belted tunic,
bare arms, goatskin, boots, staff,
except for hoods which display different symbols
for different houses.

On the river bank the monks from the weaving houses
are collecting rushes.

All work in silence.
A few look up as the boat pulls alongside
the rough landing jetty, but are quietly reproved by
supervisors and put their eyes down again.

GATE-KEEPER-MONK *comes over*
to wait for the boat as it moors at the jetty.

*Gate-keeper is clearly surprised at the presence of
two Egyptian priests, but observes the monastery's
usual formalities:*

> KEEPER
> You are welcome at the monastery of the
> confraternity of Abba Pachomius at Phbow.
> Do you require shelter, food, or assistance?

> RAMIR
> We wish to speak with Abba Theodore.

> KEEPER
> You are welcome to stay at our guest house
> as honoured visitors.
> But Abba Theodore is away at our monastery
> of Tabbenesi until this evening.

> ATHANASIUS
> *(still dressed as a servant)*
> We will wait for him here.

> KEEPER
> *(surprised at a servant speaking in this way
> but tries to hide it:)*
> Then come with me.

*Keeper shows them to the guest-house building,
smaller and no better than the rest.*

34. INT. GUEST HOUSE. CONTINUOUS.

*Ramir leads Mekhen to a rough bed to rest.
Mekhen is clearly increasingly weary from the
journey. Kador off-loads the baggage.*

*MONK-1 arrives with a jug of water and baskets
of cheese, figs, fruit, bread and salt.
He leaves these at the threshold of the guest-house.*

ATHANASIUS
(calling to departing monk)
Please bring some writing tablets.

*MONK-1 can be seen going over to the copyist group
to get writing implements.*

ATHANASIUS *(to Mekhen)*
Theodore will recognise me. The community
sent him to Alexandria to tell me of
Pachomius's death ten years ago.
Others may also recognise me.
I visited this monastery myself nearly twenty
years ago. But I should be able to lose myself
as just another anonymous monk,
until I can safely return to Alexandria.

RAMIR
I had heard of this community of monks
but didn't imagine it to be like this.

MEKHEN
Pachomius was a good man, simple, sincere.
He attracted many followers. But some are
now hostile to us. Some have tried to destroy
the ancient temples near these monasteries.

ATHANASIUS
The community has always attracted spiritual
men, but also eccentrics, and even fanatics.
There could be some unorthodox among
them. Hostile to me as well as to you.

MONK-1 returns with writing implements.
Curious, but silently hands them over to Ramir.
Who hands them to Athanasius.
Monk leaves.

> ATHANASIUS
> I can see I will have to act my part more
> carefully. As a servant. And as a monk.
> But for now I must still act as Patriarch.
> I must write to the church at Alexandria
> and to all the bishops of Egypt.
> The church must know that I am still free
> and not in the hands of the Arians.

Athanasius starts writing on a waxed tablet.

Mekhen, tired, rests.

Ramir and Kador wander out of the guest-house
to see the rest of the monastery.

35. EXT. MONASTERY COMPOUND.
EARLY EVENING.

Ramir and Kador are wandering curiously around
the compound. The Gate-keeper follows suspiciously
at a distance. As they talk, they encounter various
odd vignettes:

> KADOR
> Do you trust Athanasius?

> RAMIR
> He will keep his word.

KADOR
But will the Kom Ombo christians
obey his word?

RAMIR
If they do, it will weaken Governor Flavius.
He needs the support of the christians
as well as the backing of the garrison.

*They pass three youths praying prostrate face-down
in the dust at the gate of the compound. (These are
postulants hoping for entry into the monastery.)*

KADOR
Do you really think Governor Flavius
is trying to create an independent
little kingdom for himself?

RAMIR
I'm not sure. He would probably end up as
dependent on the Nubians as he is now on
Alexandria or Constantinople.
He needs the trading outlets, in either case.
But he's ambitious.

KADOR
At least he would weaken the Romans.

RAMIR
Would you prefer a petty tyrant
or an imperial tyrant?

KADOR
I want neither.
I want my people to rule themselves.

                    RAMIR
The Romans have been in Egypt for
four hundred years. The Greeks ruled us
for three hundred before that.

                    KADOR
And we ruled ourselves
for three thousand years before that.

                    RAMIR
Perhaps. I'm not sure who 'we' are.
My sister's husband is Nubian,
so my nephew is half-Nubian.
And I'm certainly no Pharoah.

*They stop, puzzled, to watch two monks
carrying heavy bags of sand.*

The watch for a while, then move on, as:

*One monk goes from place A to place B, leaves a bag
of sand at B, returns to A, picks up another bag of
sand, goes to B, crossing with the second monk who
picks up the bag of sand just left at B and carries it to
A, leaves it at A, returns to B, picks up the next bag
left by the first monk.*

Repeat.

*This cycle of endless repetition continues in the
background as Ramir and Kador resume walking.*

                    KADOR
Athanasius may be more dangerous
than the Governor, or even the Emperor.

                    RAMIR
          I don't see how. He's just a bishop.
          Different religion, but a priest, like me.

                    KADOR
          He's more Roman than the Romans. He wants
          his empire to cover the whole world.
          All of us under one universal god, his god.

                    RAMIR
          No religion can do that.

                    KADOR
          But religion and the sword can.
          The empire is now christian.

                    RAMIR
          I will not take up a sword
          to defeat another religion.

                    KADOR
          But to defend your people? Not all christians
          are like that cheerful monk in Alexandria.
          (points at Monk-2) Does he look friendly?

*They are near MONK-2: a large strong man with a
thick black beard, stripped to the waist, standing
tensely upright and holding his arms out rigidly,
eyes closed, praying to the sky.
A wooden cross gripped in each hand.*

*As Ramir and Kador come too near, Monk-2 opens
blazing eyes, furious at their intrusion on his space.*

                    MONK-2
          (shouts furiously) I am praying!

As Ramir backs off, Monk-2 returns to praying.

MONK-3 in nearby group of weavers
starts singing softly:

MONK-3 *(sings)*
The lord is my shepherd—

Monk-2 stops angrily, and throws a wooden cross
viciously at Monk-3.

MONK-2
I am praying!!

Weavers' SUPERVISOR intervenes, to Monk-3.

SUPERVISOR
Patience, brother.

Kador has reached for his knife under his robe.
Ramir and Kador continue walking.

RAMIR
Not all christians are like him either.

KADOR
Perhaps not yet.

RAMIR
This is supposed to be a community
of peace and brotherhood.

KADOR
All ideals corrupt.

RAMIR
Not religious ones.

KADOR
Especially religious ones.

RAMIR
So you do not want to save the temple.

KADOR
I am grateful to the temple. It has sheltered
me. But there are more important things.

*As Ramir and Kador pass a group of metal-working
monks (making a considerable hammering noise)
several monks make the sign of cross at them and
hiss:*
MONKS *(variously)*
Demons! — Idolators! — Devils-dung!!

Their supervisor does not intervene.

RAMIR
Perhaps you're right. About some things.

They continue walking in silence.

*Ramir and Kador pause before 3 whips
hanging from 3 palm-trees
outside the large central building.*

35. EXT. NEAR MONASTERY. EVENING.

*In a silent long shot ABBOT THEODORE is walking
across the desert. He is dressed as an ordinary monk.*

Theodore enters the monastery compound.
The Gate-keeper is seen telling him about the guests.

36. INT. GUEST HOUSE. CONTINUOUS

Theodore enters. Puzzled at an Egyptian High Priest,
Mekhen, lying on the bed.
Then sees and suddenly recognises Athanasius.

                    THEODORE
          My Lord Father..

                    ATHANASIUS *(interrupts him)*
          Merely a humble servant of an
          Egyptian high priest. *(smiles)*
          But one who wishes to become a simple
          monk in your monastery...

                    THEODORE
          (baffled) ??

                    ATHANASIUS
          Let me explain this small miracle
          of conversion to you..

37. INT. COMMUNAL DINING ROOM.
LATE EVENING.

The central building. Very large but bare room.
A few unglazed window apertures.
Simple tables and benches. 200 or more monks
are seated. Barefooted. In silence.
Theodore presides but the 'high table' arrangement
is not very prominent.

Food is distributed onto tables
by three MONK-COOKS.

First to the high table. Just bread and water.
Theodore is surprised at the meagre fare.
Meal continues. Bread and water for everyone.

Theodore turns to his deputy,
ABBOT PLENES, *at his side.*

> THEODORE
> Has something happened while I was away?
> A fire in the storehouses?

> PLENES
> We have not had vegetables or porridge
> since you left, Abba.
> The cooks say they are economising.

Theodore calls the three cooks over.

> THEODORE
> This is not a day of fasting?

> COOK-1
> No, Abba.

> THEODORE
> Abba Plenes says you are economising.
> Is that so?

> COOK-2
> We have saved some money.
> To give to the poor.

THEODORE
Is that not the responsibility of the steward?
Your task is to cook for the brethren.

COOK-3
We have also saved time.
To make more mats. To sell for the poor.

THEODORE
That is the business of the bursar.
Not the kitchen.

COOK-1
(hesitates—finally :)
We think the brethren are too lax, too
indulgent. They should fast more, not less.

THEODORE
So you make that decision for them. *(pause)*
Bring me the mats you say you made for the
poor when you should have been cooking for
the brethren.

*Cooks go to the kitchen. Whole room is now eyeing
events. Cooks quickly return with mats. About a
dozen rush mats, thinly and rather poorly woven.*

THEODORE
Burn them. *(pause)* Here. Now.

*Cook-1 almost disobeys.
Finally he gets a fire-brand from the kitchen.*

*The Cooks sullenly burn the mats in the middle
of the large room. Smoke rises and belches
out of the windows.*

38. INT. GUEST HOUSE. CONTINUOUS.

*Ramir, Mekhen, Kador and Athanasius have finished
a simple meal in the guest-house. Athanasius is
writing again. Mekhen and Kador are both stretched
out, tired.*

*Ramir looks out of the doorway and sees the smoke
coming from the windows of the communal hall.
Puzzled.*

*Ramir leaves the guest-house and goes to the hall.
Outside are 200 pairs of battered boots.
200 wooden staffs. The 3 palm trees with whips.*

*Ramir stands outside but looks in, unseen,
to see why smoke is coming out. Baffled.*

*He stays listening to the following.
Occasionally cut to his watching reactions.*

39. INT. COMMUNAL HALL.

*Theodore has waited till the mats are ash.
Then he stands.
He delivers the following quietly,
as a normal evening homily.
Monks continue eating bread and water throughout.*

> THEODORE
> May the peace of god be with you.

> ALL MONKS IN UNISON
> And with you.

THEODORE
May the blessing of God
and all the saints come down upon us.
May we all come to salvation.

ALL MONKS IN UNISON
Amen.

THEODORE

My sons—

Through the first part of the speech,
camera shows reaction shots from the cooks:
two cooks remain resentful, but one is reconciled.

THEODORE
Fire cleanses all rust
and makes an object shine.
When a man has something
and abstains from it for the sake of God,
he gains a great reward.
But to force others to abstain is to deprive
them of their reward for abstaining.
When you give bread and you have
plenty of it, are you being truly good?
When you have no fruit so do not eat it,
are you being truly good?
Do not have much and give little.
Have little and give much.
So the fire of god cleanses all evil from us.
 (pause)

From here, close-up shots of the varied faces of
monks: wrinkled, young, tired, spiritual, bitter, sour.

My sons,
Before he died, our founding father,
Pachomius, had a vision.
He saw in his vision a great black pit
with a tall pillar in the middle,
reaching to the sky but blocking out the light.
And many men were in the pit,
unable to see where to go to find the light.
Some went round and round the pillar,
thinking they were going to the light.
Then our father Pachomius saw in his vision
that our community was also in the darkness.
But they were following a lamp.
Only four of the brethren could see the lamp
and they followed it.
But the rest followed
behind those four brethren,
each holding onto his neighbour's shoulder,
because they were in the darkness.
If one let go, all those behind him went astray.
Guided by the lamp in this way,
they came to an opening
and saw the way to the great light above.

(pause. then ritual ending:)

Pray for your father Theodore
who has sinned.
Pray for your brethren who have sinned.
Amen.

ALL MONKS IN UNISON
Amen.

Theodore pauses. Different tone:

                    THEODORE
          My sons, we have guests.
          Make them welcome. But do not be curious.
          Pray for them.

40. EXT. OUTSIDE HALL. NOW DUSK.

As the homily ends, Ramir slips away quietly,
back to the guest-house.

The 200 monks begin to file out from the hall.

Each puts on a pair of boots and takes a staff
from those outside the door.
They do not choose which boots or staff.
They go in ordered lines to their respective houses.
In total silence.

41. INT. GUEST HOUSE. DEEP NIGHT.

Mekhen, Kador and Athanasius are asleep.
Ramir also asleep, but tossing and turning.
Moonlight.

42. DREAM SEQUENCE.

Ramir's nightmare: Rapid, almost subliminal, lurid,
very violent scenes.
Echoes of the earlier flash insert:

        The harlot Pelagia on a horse, naked,
        but merges rapidly into the woman from the
        basilica being skewered with a sword.

        But now her face is that of the woman attacked
        by a crocodile in the earlier flash insert.

Huge figure of Nonnus laughing at Ramir.
Nonnus in a rage shouts: "I am praying!"
and hurls a great wooden cross at Ramir.

Monks being whipped. Tied to palm trees.

Human torches flaming in public gardens.

Egyptian gods: hawk, ibis, jackal,
tearing at living human bodies.

Temple on fire. Smoke choking.

Men including Ramir groping blind
round a pillar in darkness.

Naked men and women in gold mines,
in smoke and fire.

Repeat of the flash insert of crocodile
attacking terrified woman.
Churning water. Blood. Woman's face
in horror as she is savaged by crocodile.

Repeat Egyptian animal-gods tearing at flesh.
Crocodiles churning in water under moon.

Crocodile is devouring the woman.

Ramir falls backwards from a boat
into the black waters of the Nile.

Huge crocodile snaps at him—

Ramir wakes from the dream. Terrified.
A dawn gong is summoning the monks to prayer.

43. INT. GUEST HOUSE. MORNING.

Athanasius, now dressed as an ordinary monk,
is writing. Several tablets already written.
Theodore is waiting for him to finish.
Theodore is talking to Mekhen.
Ramir and Kador not present.

>   MEKHEN
> May I ask you something?
> Since you give yourselves to so much
> hardness and abstinence, prayer and vigils,
> even chastity and poverty,
> is it so that you can receive
> visions of your god?

>   THEODORE
> No. I have never seen God.

>   MEKHEN *(simply)*
> Yet when we enter the sanctuary of our god,
> and make an offering to him,
> he hides nothing from us and discloses his
> mysteries to us. Even to this blind believer.
> Yet you say that you see nothing.

>   THEODORE
> God has revealed himself only in his Son.

>   MEKHEN *(puzzled, not hostile)*
> Whom you have never seen. Or heard.
> *(pause)*
> If you see nothing, is it because you have
> unworthy images in your hearts which come
> between you and your god? Is it for this
> reason his mysteries are not revealed to you?

THEODORE
(silent)

ATHANASIUS
Finished.

Athanasius stops writing.
He hands writing tablets to Theodore.

ATHANASIUS
Ninety copies. Please. As soon as possible.

44. EXT. COMPOUND.

Theodore exits. He goes across the compound
to the copyists group. He hands tablets to the
supervisor, who distributes work.

45. INT. GUEST HOUSE.

ATHANASIUS *(to Mekhen)*
You would have got along well with
Abba Pachomius.

MEKHEN *(pause)*
Will you write to the Bishop of Kom Ombo?

ATHANASIUS
I am writing to all the bishops.
They must know that I am not dead yet.
(pause) Yes, I will write to the Bishop of
Kom Ombo. Your temple will not become a
christian church.

Athanasius writes a further note.

46. EXT. OUTSIDE COPYISTS HUT.

Twenty monk copyists outside their hut, in a row.
Squatting in the traditional Egyptian scribe position.

Athanasius brings the new note himself
over to the copyists. Hands it to the supervisor.

> ATHANASIUS
> One copy please.

Athanasius notices the scrolls which the
COPYIST-SUPERVISOR himself has been copying.

Picks up one. Reads it casually.
Then seriously. Picks up two others.
Scans them. Looks at supervisor.

> ATHANASIUS
> A local customer?

> COPYIST-SUPERVISOR
> Some of the brethren. *(uneasy pause)*
> They read them to refute them.

> ATHANASIUS
> I see.

Athanasius heads towards Theodore's house.

Supervisor waits till Athanasius is out of hearing.
Calls over two copyists.

He hands them a dozen scrolls
that Athanasius hasn't actually looked at.

                    COPYIST-SUPERVISOR
          Peios, Sourous, these need to disappear.
          Urgently.

Peios & Sourous take the scrolls,
put them into a bag. They walk quickly away.

47. EXT. MONASTERY. RIVER BANK. DAY.

At the jetty. Farewell embraces between
Theodore and Athanasius, who are staying,
and Ramir, Mekhen and Kador,
who are leaving in the boat.

                    A COPYIST *(shouts from a distance)*
          The cross has conquered!
          Victory will be ours!

                    THEODORE *(sharply)*
          Brother!

Theodore goes to reprove the copyist.
Athanasius is silent.
As they embark, only Ramir and Kador notice
Christian graffiti scrawled on the side of the boat:
a cross and a Xi-Ro sign.
Ramir says nothing to Mekhen.

                    KADOR *(to Ramir)*
          The boat will need cleaning
          when we get home.

The boat swings away into the river,
heading up river, south.

48. EXT. RIVER NILE. CONTINUOUS.

*The camera pulls back to a high aerial helicopter
shot, with the boat at first in the centre of the shot
as it moves out into the river.*

*Then a long zoom onto the river-bank
just beyond the monastery.*

*In long shot, Peios and Sourous can be seen placing
scrolls into jars and burying jars in a cave in the side
of the cliff (at Nag Hammadi).*

49. EXT. RIVER NILE. CONTINUOUS.

*Ramir, Mekhen and Kador on boat sailing upstream.
Hold on shot briefly.*

50. EXT. MONASTERY JETTY.
ALMOST CONTINUOUS.

*The boat is out of sight.
Athanasius is no longer on the jetty.*

*A boat arrives from the north,
with a Roman officer and a small troop of soldiers.
Officer and soldiers disembark.
Soldiers line up near jetty.*

*Officer is greeted by Gate-keeper.
Theodore is nearby.*

              KEEPER *(ritual)*
You are welcome at the monastery of the
confraternity of Abba Pachomius at Phbow.
Do you require shelter, food, or assistance?

OFFICER
I have reason to believe that the renegade
Athanasius has taken refuge
in one of these monasteries.
My orders are to find him.

Theodore has heard and comes over. Pause.

Theodore signals to the Gate-Keeper,
who strikes the gong, once. Then continuously.

THEODORE *(to Officer)*
Certainly you may search for the Patriarch
Athanasius among my monks.
There are a thousand in this monastery.
And nine more monasteries.
You do know what he looks like?

As the gong sounds continuously,
all the monks in the various work groups stand
and start to walk towards the jetty.

Scores more monks also come out of all the huts at
once. All identically dressed. Hooded, carrying their
staves. They move in a slowly converging phalanx,
towards the troops.

The officer and soldiers back away.

OFFICER
We will be back.

THEODORE
And we will be here.

Officer and soldiers retreat to their boat to leave.

51. EXT. RIVER NILE.
LATE EVENING. NEAR SUN-SET.
(between Denderah and Edfu]

Boat is steered by Kador.
Making good progress under sail.
Some scattered small-boat traffic on river.
Mainly heading south.

There is a slightly festive air on some boats,
a few are even decorated.
Occasional instrumental music from passing boats.
Evening sun slanting across. Peaceful.

Ramir and Mekhen are seated under an awning.

        MEKHEN
(suddenly realising:)
The Feast of Joyous Union!
The goddess Hathor will be
on her way to Edfu.

        RAMIR
Yes, it's nearly the full moon.

        MEKHEN
I haven't been to the festival since my eyes
failed. You took my place. Ten years.

        RAMIR
I asked Sekhet to represent Kom Ombo this
year. I thought we would not be back in time.

        MEKHEN
I remember the first time I saw the great
barge. As a child.

We would line the banks.
Be there before dawn to find a spot.
And the sacred boats would come round
the great bend of the river
and the goddess would be golden in the sun,
going to her god.
I can still see it, in my mind. *(pause)*
In the last year of his life,
my father was Mayor of our small town.
He was so proud.
Greeting the goddess as she passed.
Then joining the long line of great barges
from Dendera, Thebes, Esna.
All the way to Edfu. *(pause)*
I thought of him the first time
I represented our temple at the festival.

Mekhen falls silent.

Their boat continues round a bend in the river.
The river is wide at this point.
There are a few scattered people
watching from the banks.
Ahead is a group of four smallish boats.

As the boat approaches the small flotilla
we see the sacred barge of Hathor in the centre.
Faded gold paint. Neglected. Dilapidated.
Towed by two row-boats.
Minimal rowing crew in each.

The sacred barge of the goddess Hathor is making
the annual pilgrimage to the temple at Edfu with the
goddess on board. But the festival procession is not
what it was.

*The enthroned statue of the goddess is visible
on the barge. Hathor is the cow goddess,
a woman with the ears of a cow, the Goddess of love,
music, and dance.*

*There are only a few priests on the barge, all elderly.
Only one musician, not even playing.
Some provincial dignitaries in the one following
boat. All look weary. They are twelve days into the
ritual annual journey from Denderah.*

*Ramir hopes Mekhen will not realise
they are passing such a run-down sight.*

*Ramir looks at Kador.
Ramir puts his finger to his lips to be quiet.
Kador makes a silent gesture,
indicating he will steer very wide to pass.*

*But as the boat passes nearest the barge
Mekhen hears the slap of water and becomes alert.
Listening but cannot see.
Ramir quickly intervenes. He lies.*

> RAMIR
> We might just catch up with the great
> procession before they moor tonight.
> The river is getting more crowded
> with pilgrim boats heading that way.
> We can't be too far behind.

Kador and Ramir exchange glances.

Kador anticipates a problem, which comes:

            MEKHEN
We could moor at Edfu
and wait for the ceremony?

            RAMIR *(thinks quickly)*
We would lose too much time.
The temple will be vulnerable
while so many of our people are
here at the festival.

            KADOR *(encouragingly)*
If we sail through the night
we can be home tomorrow.

            MEKHEN *(reluctantly)*
You're right. I don't trust Governor Flavius.
He might choose just this time to strike.

            RAMIR
The sooner we get there now, the better.

            MEKHEN
Yes. I'm tired. Time for home.

Mekhen relaxes back.
He starts singing softly, almost to himself.

            MEKHEN *sings:*
When the stars give way to the Sun-boat
As it sails on the Nile of the Sky
I shall go with Ra on his journey—

52. EXT. RIVER NILE. SUNSET INTO NIGHT.

Song continues gently as voice-over
while the boat passes Edfu in the dark.

MEKHEN *(sings, voice-over)*
—The breezes will blow so softly
To guide the Boat on its way
As it sails to the western horizon
In peace at the close of the day.

Then Wisdom shall be at the tiller
And Righteousness stand at the prow
And Ra shall abide in his glory.

There are no crowds. No sign of a festival at all.
Lights of the town as reflections in the water.
Very quiet.

Abrupt sound and visuals cut to:

53. EXT. KOM OMBO. TEMPLE.
BRIGHT DAYLIGHT.

Sudden loud crash as a wooden catapult engine
hurls a large stone at the wall of the double temple
of Kom Ombo.

The temple looks as if it has already suffered
a continuous pounding.

54. EXT. UPON TEMPLE WALLS.

On the walls of the temple are about
20 determined workers. Young and old.
Stonemasons, carvers, builders, painters,
from the temple workshops.
Armed with their tools. They have fortified
the narrow entrance. Silent. Grim.

Among the workers are PANIB,
a black Nubian male, about 35,
and SEKHET, *a priest, about 60.*

Another stone crashes into the wall.
Not much damage.

55. EXT. KOM OMBO.
AREA OUTSIDE THE TEMPLE.

About 80 Roman troops. In full battle gear.
Awaiting the assault order.
Large wooden seige catapult to one side.
Throws a third stone.

56. EXT. AREA OUTSIDE THE TEMPLE.

A crowd of about two hundred local townspeople
is looking on from behind a cordon of a few troops.
The crowd is between the temple area
and the landing stage.
Mainly women at the front of the crowd.

A paused stand-off between troops, workers, crowd.
Crowd is currently passive and uncertain.

57. EXT. AREA OUTSIDE THE TEMPLE.

A group of officers and dignitaries are assembled,
talking quietly.

Two senior legionary OFFICERS,
professional soldiers.

Two local SENATORS,
provincial politicians-landowners.

NEBRE, *the High Priest of the Temple of Sobek.*
He is aged about 50.
Prosperous. Affable. Unflappable. Opportunist.

GOVERNOR GAIUS FLAVIUS, *in late 40's.*
A schemer and a gambler.
Sharp. Impatient, but a canny survivor.

BISHOP AMENIUS, *worldly*
but actually out of his depth.

They are all dressed without much regalia.
Mainly in everyday Roman costume, well-worn togas
or uniform. Practical and experienced men,
provincial, but ambitious. Not fools.

Discussion is relaxed. Business-like attitude.

This assault is seen by them as a fairly minor matter,
to be concluded without fuss.

But they also see it as part of a larger project.
The Governor is firmly in charge.

> OFFICER-1 *(to Governor)*
> We can take it, of course, Governor. But not
> without loss. They're quite well dug in.

> SENATOR-1
> How much blood?
> Some of that crowd still think it's sacred.
> They won't want blood shed in there.

                    BISHOP
Nor would I, obviously.

                    GOVERNOR
Don't be squeamish, my Lord Bishop.
You can always re-consecrate it,
or whatever you do, after you have it.

                    BISHOP
Not if you reduce it to rubble first.
The idea was to have a resource, not a ruin.

                    GOVERNOR
That's your problem. I don't like being defied.
I want a victory. Visible. Final.
No more resistance.

                    SENATOR-2 *(ironic)*
"The Cross Has Conquered.
Victory Will Be Ours."

                    GOVERNOR *(to Officer-1)*
Commander, let's see how seriously
they feel about it. Probe them a bit.

                    OFFICER-1
Yessir.

The two officers go off to organise an assault.

58. EXT. RIVER NILE NEAR KOM OMBO.

*View from Ramir's boat as it draws near to Kom
Ombo. The double temple is visible on the rise above
the river as the boat rounds a bend.
They see the catapult in action. Alarmed.*

59. EXT. AREA OUTSIDE THE TEMPLE.

*A foot-soldier assault on the temple proceeds
during the following exchanges.
Low-key, exploratory and tactical assault.
More like a police operation against a factory
occupation. But some brief fierce hand to hand.
Defenders repulse attackers.
Minor wounded on both sides.*

*The assault is visible mainly as background action.
But there are occasional cuts between the action and
the discussion.
Dignitaries continue in fairly relaxed coversation,
with half an eye on the action.*

SENATOR-2
Not going to be that easy.

BISHOP *(to High Priest Nebre)*
I thought we had an agreement, Nebre.
You didn't expect this?

NEBRE *(shrugs)*
It's mainly Mekhen's workmen.
My lot did as they were told.

SENATOR-1
Perhaps we should just use the big seige
engine. Knock it down around them.

NEBRE
Maybe. But it took two hundred years
to build. It'll take more than a few days
to knock it down.

GOVERNOR
Point taken, Nebre.
Any more useful contributions?

NEBRE
Just walk away. Another two hundred years it
will have fallen down by itself. From neglect.

GOVERNOR *(drily)*
A rather longer timetable than
the one I had in mind.

NEBRE
Tell them you're going to build a new one.

GOVERNOR
(looks startled) ??

NEBRE
These families have had generations
of work on this site.
They don't want to be out of a job.
So promise them something new to work on.
A big christian basilica on some other site
would do the trick. They'll switch gods
if there's steady building work to be done.
I know them.

SENATOR-2
Meanwhile, they seem pretty committed
to the old gods.

NEBRE
Not really. They want the old Egypt.
They confuse that with the old gods.
They just don't like change.

SENATOR-1
Well they can't avoid it.
The empire's gone christian.

BISHOP *(interposes)*
Even if for the moment
it's the wrong kind of christian.

GOVERNOR
But our new christian friends to the south
are just the right kind, Bishop.
The Nubians have gold, slaves, camels.
And we have the market for them.
A merger made in heaven.
I want one market, one state, one temple.
Or church. And I shall get it.

SENATOR-2
And one little caesar?

GOVERNOR
One step at a time, senator.

Officer-1 comes to report back to Governor.

OFFICER-1
They seem pretty serious about it,sir.

GOVERNOR
So I see. Call a halt.
It's going to be a long day.

*Nebre sees Ramir, Mekhen, and Kador
disembarking in the distance.*

NEBRE
It just got longer.

60. EXT. KOM OMBO. NEAR LANDING STAGE.
CONTINUOUS.

The boat has landed.
Ramir, Mekhen, and Kador disembark.
Kador leads Mekhen through the crowd
towards the temple area.
Kador is explaining the situation to Mekhen.
Crowd obviously respect Mekhem a lot.

Ramir is embraced by his sister, SHEFRU.
(She is married to PANIB, *worker-leader on the*
wall.) Their 7 year old son, KHEM, *is with her.*
He has a small wooden sword.

SHEFRU
We were hoping you would get back
before it started, brother.

RAMIR
We did the best we could, Shefru.

SHEFRU
Success?

MEKHEN *(overhears and joins them)*
We have official letters from
the Imperial Prefect himself and from
the High Priest of All Egypt.

RAMIR
Where is Panib?

                    SHEFRU
          Up on the temple wall, of course.
          Determined to stop this.
          Even Khem wanted to be with his father.

She smiles down at her son's wooden sword.

                    RAMIR
          How many?

                    SHEFRU
          (optimistic) Thirty?

                    RAMIR
          Not enough. We need a lot more support.

                    MEKHEN
          It's time to talk, Ramir.
          Please, take me to the Governor.

Ramir and Mekhen proceed towards the temple area.

*The soldiers are clearly under orders
to let the priests through.
Some soldiers form a semi-escort around them,
not quite arresting them.*

*But the soldiers make Shefru and Khem
stay back with the rest of the crowd.*

61. EXT. TEMPLE AREA. CONTINUOUS.

*Ramir and Mekhen have reached the group of
dignitaries.*

GOVERNOR
High Priest of Horus,
I hear you have been to Alexandria.
Neglecting your temple.

MEKHEN
Protecting my temple. I have an order for you.
From Imperial Prefect Maximus of All Egypt.

Ramir hands the letter to Governor
who glances through it. Not over-concerned.

GOVERNOR
Well, these officials come and go.
Unfortunately for you, Mekhen,
the imperial post travels faster than an old
Nile boat. I have already been informed that
Imperial Prefect Maximus is being replaced.
A bungled operation, I gather.
Some attack on a church that went a bit
wrong. Prominent citizens roughed up.
Even the famous Madame Pelagia.
I gather she was not pleased. I'll have to
check with the new man, of course.
But not till we've settled this little business.

Mekhen is nonplussed. Ramir intervenes.

RAMIR
We also have another letter. For you, bishop.

Ramir hands Bishop Amenius the letter
from Athanasius. Bishop reads. Baffled.

BISHOP
From Athanasius? How did you get this?
We heard he was in hiding.
Or arrested.

RAMIR
A small miracle. Or two.

BISHOP
(shows letter to Governor.)
I can't go against that.

GOVERNOR
Athanasius is no longer Patriarch.
George of Cappadocia is.

BISHOP
George is a heretic condemned by my church.
I do not recognise him.

GOVERNOR
George is the Patriarch of Alexandria,
approved by my government.
I firmly suggest that you recognise him,
at least tactically, for now.

RAMIR
Which government would that be, Flavius?
The Emperor's or your very own?

GOVERNOR
The Emperor has not been replaced. Yet.
And it is on his authority
that I am closing this temple.

RAMIR
As a prelude to holding that very emperor to
ransom once you fully control this region.

GOVERNOR
Never even considered it.
Are you suggesting rebellion against the
Emperor?I thought you might have been
rather keen on that.

RAMIR
Why should I leave a sinking barge
for a sinking canoe?

(tense pause)

GOVERNOR
I think we all need time for some quiet
reflection. *(to Mekhen)*
Mekhen, I will give you one hour to persuade
those people of yours to leave the temple.
After that we pound it to rubble.
Officer, escort the high priest to his temple.
For the last time.
*(to Ramir)*You stay here.
(to Mekhen) If you don't return
within the hour, Ramir is executed.

62. EXT. TEMPLE AREA. CONTINUOUS.

Mekhen is led off by Officer towards the temple.
During the following exchange we see Mekhen in the
background being let into the temple, after a brief
exchange between the officer and defenders.

Ramir stands next to Nebre.

Rest of the dignitaries are quietly bored.

Troops are stood down.

        RAMIR
My Lord High Priest of the Temple of Sobek,
perhaps you would tell me why you are
out here with Romans and Christians
and not in your temple defending it?

        NEBRE *(not unkindly)*
Ramir, when I was your age there were
30 priests and 300 workers in that temple.
A hundred years ago, it would have been
300 priests and a thousand workers.
It's coming to an end. Let it go.
There are new gods to follow. I'm a realist.

        RAMIR
The end of four thousand years?
You really think so, Nebre?
But your gods were never really
the gods of Egypt.
Just the corrupt gods of gold and power.
Realist? You're simply backing a new winner.
You hope.

        NEBRE
We'll see. Mekhen and I never really agreed.
Though I do have a lot of respect for him.
The whole town does.
But that doesn't mean they still believe
in the old ways. Does anybody?

63. EXT. INSIDE TEMPLE.

*Mekhen makes his way through the narrow gap
opened up by defending workers in the barricades.*

*He pauses to finger (blind) some incised
hieroglyphics on the wall.
Reads them with his fingertips. Murmurs a prayer:*

>   MEKHEN
> Shining Eye of Horus, come to our aid.
> Ibis, god of foresight and wisom, help me.

*Mekhen is taken up onto the walls to meet the
defenders. He picks his blind way sure-footedly.
The defences are meagre:
stacked stones, chisels, hammers.
The leader is Panib, husband of Shefru.
He is black. Nubian. Solid. 35. Stonemason.
A Craftsman. He greets Mekhen.*

>   MEKHEN
> How long can you hold out, Panib?

>   PANIB
> We can't. We were only trying to delay it
> until you got back from Alexandria.

>   SEKHET
> We thought Flavius would only strike
> once the festival started at Edfu.
> But we didn't take any chances.

>   MEKHEN
> Is that you, Sekhet? So nobody went to Edfu.
> That's why it seemed so quiet.

                    WORKER-2
We moved in as soon as you left.
They got a surprise when they attacked
the following morning.

                    WORKER-3
But then they started to use the siege catapult.
You can see the damage it's already done.

Mekhen smiles wryly at the word 'see'.
His smile says both: 'I wish I could'
and 'I'm glad I can't'.

                    PANIB
                (covering the mistake)
It's only a matter of time.

64. EXT. TEMPLE AREA.

Ramir and Nebre are still standing together.

                    RAMIR
I have another letter. For you.
(Hands him a letter]

                    NEBRE *(sees the seal)*
The High Priest of All Egypt. How nice of
him. You have been busy. *(reads)*
So now you're Deputy to both of us.
Right of succession to both shrines.
Congratulations. Well, it was always pretty
expensive having two priest-hoods.
Time to consolidate. One temple, two gods.
One god, two temples. Whatever works.
As he says, it's hard to get the right staff
these days.

                    RAMIR
I am willing to serve both sanctuaries.

                    NEBRE
I haven't resigned. Yet.
My business arrangements with our dear
governor may, after all, need some
renegotiating. If he screws this up.
I might need the old job to fall back on.

65. EXT. AREA OUTSIDE TEMPLE.
TIME HAS PASSED.

                    GOVERNOR *(to Officer)*
They've had enough time. Catapult first.
Then rush them. No quarter.
I want this over and done with.

Officer proceeds to order the catapult to fire.
Catapult fires one large stone.
Another is being primed.
Troops take up assault positions.

66. EXT. WALL OF TEMPLE

Suddenly Mekhen appears
on the highest point on the wall, alone.

                    MEKHEN *(loud voice)*
In the name of Horus, and of Sobek,
the ancient gods of Egypt.
In the name of Zeus and Venus,
and the gods of Rome.
In the name of the Father, Son and Spirit,
the gods of the christians.
Listen.

He has everyone's attention.
Everybody pauses. Soldiers uncertain.
Crowd, still behind the now distracted cordon
of a few soldiers, try to see.
Pause.

Mekhen advances one step,
now dangerously near the edge of the wall.

MEKHEN *(loud voice)*
The time has come.

He steps forward.
And apparently misses his footing.
He falls forward off the high wall
into the area outside the temple.
Hits the ground. Blood. Dead.
The body lies there.

67. EXT. AREA BEFORE TEMPLE WALL.
CONTINUOUS.

Crowd is horrified and surges forward,
breaking through the barrier of soldiers.
The crowd is led by women,
Shefru prominently visible,
with Khem waving his wooden sword but in tears.

The crowd now overwhelms the troops by sheer
numbers. The catapult is also surrounded.
No actual fighting but close-hand intermingling
which makes it impossible for the troops to re-
organise.

Kador contrives to capture a soldier's sword.

                    GOVERNOR
Damn him. Now we'll have a full scale riot
on our hands. *(furious, to Officer)*
This needs to be defused. Immediately.
Get them back to barracks.
There's always another day.

Governor stalks away.
Officers marshall the troops to return to barracks.
Crowd gathers round the body of Mekhen.
Ramir and Nebre are still at the fringe of the melée.

                    NEBRE
So what, in the name of all those gods,
was he going to say?

                    RAMIR
He said it.

Nebre looks puzzled.

                    RAMIR
He may have been blind.
But his feet knew every inch of that temple.

                    NEBRE *(pause)*
I see. He always did know how to handle
a crowd. A fine rhetorician.

                    RAMIR
You don't always need words.

                    NEBRE
So, it will fall to me to instruct you
in your new duties.

                    RAMIR
          My first duty is to bury him. *(pause)*
          In the old ways.

68. EXT. KOM OMBO.
EARLY MORNING LIGHT.

*A high camera shot follows the cortege of Mekhen
as it winds through the small town to the landing
stage. The ceremonial boat of burial is carried by
priests and workers.
On the boat is the linen-wrapped shroud of Mekhen.
The whole town follows to the landing stage.*

*We see Nebre (NB: not Ramir) begin to recite
a prayer at the landing stage.*

*As the prayer proceeds it becomes
Nebre's voice-over at (+++)
while the rest of the scene proceeds visually
but not in real-time. Several lap-dissolves.*

                    NEBRE *(ritualistically)*
          May he repose in the Western Mountain,
          and come forth on the earth
          to see the disc of the Sun.
          And may the roads be open before him
          to the high Spirit in the nether world. (+++]

          May it be granted him to enter
          as a living soul,
          to give offerings to the shining Eye of Horus,
          to Hathor princess of the Desert,
          to Osiris the great God,
          to Anubis, Lord of the Sacred Land.

        That they may grant to him
        the breathing of the sweet breezes
        of the North Wind.

While the prayer continues,
over dissolves and cuts as necessary:
a small group escort the body on a ceremonial boat
across the Nile to the west bank.

High shot: cortege carries body into desert.

                NEBRE *(voice-over continues)*
        May he cross over the firmament,
        and draw near to the great God,
        may the desert open to him her arms
        and the West hold out to him her hands.

The cortege is by now some way into the desert
on the west bank of the Nile.

        May he be welcomed
        by the Great Ones of Abydos.
        Upon the pathways of the West
        may he go in peace to the horizon
        where Osiris lives
        and may offerings be made to him
        in the desert places—

Prayer fades.

Only desert wind on the soundtrack. Bleak desert.

In a very high long shot: tiny figure of Ramir
is now alone with the linen-wrapped body
in the vast desert.
Rest of the procession has gone.

*In long shot: Ramir simply buries Mekhen
as in the very earliest burials, in the sand.
No shelter, no grave-gifts.*

*Then in medium shot:
Ramir stands silently, perhaps praying.*

Slow fade.

69. EXT. INSIDE KOM OMBO TEMPLE.
LATE AFTERNOON LIGHT.

*(Some days later)
Ramir is walking round the Temple with Nebre,
being instructed in his new duties.*

*Throughout the following scenes, some bustle and
noise as a few workers are visible at various points,
making somewhat half-hearted repairs
to the damage from the catapult.
Straight cuts between various locations.
Rapidly paced set of scenes.
Lightly comic in tone:*

70. EXT. AT NILOMETER. [A LARGE
CIRCULAR HOLE IN GROUND. EXTANT]

   RAMIR
Mekhen never wanted to be responsible
for the Nile-measuring ceremony.
He always left it to you.

   NEBRE
You can't avoid it any longer. *(slight pause)*
You do know how it works?

                    RAMIR
Of course. The solstice. We measure the
height of the Nile to predict the yearly level.
A high flood means a good year
for the farmer. A low flood a poor year.
Taxes are set accordingly for the coming year.

                    NEBRE
Mmm. That's not *quite* how it works.

                    RAMIR
I know we can get it wrong.
The Nile is nature, unpredictable.

                    NEBRE
Maybe. *(pause)*
But taxes can't afford to be unpredictable.
So, first, the Governor decides what level
of taxes the budget needs.
Then we measure. Adjusting as required.
Then we announce the height.
You'll notice the small sluice gate in the wall.
We do occasionally need to assist
nature's unpredictable ways.
It is a public ceremony, after all.

                    RAMIR *(pause)*
I can see why Mekhen declined
the honour of presiding.

                    NEBRE
He still benefitted, of course. *(pause)*
The Governor recognises that this is a
somewhat expensive service for us to provide.
Why do you think the temple's own taxes
are so low, even now?

That's one reason the christians wanted
this site for their basilica. They'd be only too
pleased to take over measuring the Nile.
For a suitable tax concession, of course.

71. EXT. 'EARS & EYES' ORACLE.
[RELIEF ON REAR WALL. EXTANT.]

Nebre and Ramir are standing before the relief.
Ramir is looking up at it.

                    RAMIR
This I rather dread. Even Mekhen doubted
his wisdom, or inspiration, at times.

                    NEBRE
Well, the oracle is one of the few services
we offer that is still reasonably popular.

                    RAMIR
But how, really, does one know the answers?
We don't even know the questions.

                    NEBRE
It's fairly simple, really.
(points to a section of the wall by the relief)
The petitioner comes here, yes,
while we stay at the front of the temple.
They whisper their question to the god.
Then come back to the front.
And we give the god's answer.
Impressive. Worth a contribution.

                    RAMIR
Not if we get it wildly wrong.

NEBRE
We don't. The questions are pretty standard.
Most people get tongue-tied,
face to face with a god.
So my assistant on duty here is happy to
suggest some suitable formulations.
 It's rare for anyone to make up their own.
Then—look down, not up—
(points to a small aperture in the wall)
 my other assistant, behind there,
listens to which one they've chosen,
or if they've said something a bit original,
and off he trots, through the tunnel, to tell me.
I have a few minutes before the petitioner
gets back to the front.
Then I give the standard, nicely ambiguous,
reply to that particular formula.
Of course, you're on your own
if the petitioner actually tries to make up his
own question. It's then the job of junior back
here to delay him a bit longer while you think
up something appropriate. But you usually
know the answer they really want to hear.
Practice makes it easy.

RAMIR
You mentioned a tunnel?

NEBRE
(Looks at him, genuinely surprised)
Mekhen really was extraordinary! Follow me.

*Nebre shows Ramir the tunnel that runs from the
oracle under the temple to the front where the priest
sat to deliver oracular answers.
Ramir looks more thoughtful.*

NEBRE
Of course, it's going to be a bit
more difficult without any junior staff.
I hear even Sekhet is leaving you.

72. INT. INSIDE CROCODILE HOUSE. DARK.

*There are three or four mummified or dessicated
crocodiles. The Crocodile god Sobek is visible in
carved wall reliefs.*

NEBRE
This is the bit you never had anything
to do with. Sobek, the crocodile god.
Your new master.

RAMIR
(remains silent)

NEBRE
(pause— puzzled at his silence.)
Of course, the peasants still believe
they come to the temple to die.
I'll show you the trap later.
We've only got one in there at the moment.
We normally starve them. It's less trouble.
And leaves fewer marks.
Though they get really ravenous.
Dangerous beasts.

RAMIR
I know. It was one of your starved beasts—

NEBRE
(suddenly dawns) Of course. Your wife.
(pause) I'm afraid I had forgotten. I am sorry.

73. EXT. AT FRONT OF TEMPLE. EVENING.

                    NEBRE
That's all. The Governor will want to see you,
of course.

                    RAMIR
He's your employer, Nebre, not mine.

                    NEBRE
Be sensible. You can work with him.

                    RAMIR
When do you actually leave?

                    NEBRE
The new gold depository won't be finished
till early next month.
Then I take over as superintendent.

                    RAMIR
I'm sure you'll find it profitable.

                    NEBRE *(kindly)*
You're living in the past, you know, Ramir.
You still want the old Egypt, the old gods.
You even want to get rid of the Empire,
the new gods. Waste of energy.
The real power is where it always was. Gold.
Respects no frontiers, no mere politicians,
no passing beliefs. Trade, the market, gold,
slaves, incense. These last.
Even in your terms, you can do far more good
if you control the market than you can with
this set of tricks.

RAMIR *(pause)*
Have you ever actually been down
the gold mines? Seen it for yourself.

NEBRE *(slight pause)*
No need to. Not my end of the business.

They stand against the darkening sky,
looking towards the sunset over the Nile
from the temple. Slow fade.

74. INT. BASILICA.

Written:]

BASILICA OF ST THEONAS,
ALEXANDRIA.
DECEMBER 24TH, 361 C.E.

Darkness lit by flaming torches.

The badly beaten and bleeding body
of George the Cappadocian
is being dragged across the floor of the basilica
by an exultant christian mob.
They are chanting:
"ATHAN-ASIUS! ATHAN-ASIUS!"

75. INT. BASILICA.

Written:]

BASILICA OF ST THEONAS,
ALEXANDRIA.
FEBRUARY 21ST 362 C.E.

Sunlight is streaming through.

Athanasius is in the pulpit.
Triumphalist cope and trappings.

An immensely enthusiastic and noisy crowd
packs the basilica, singing Psalm 136
(refrain: "His mercy endureth for ever").

Focus in on two figures in the crowd.

They are Pelagia, dressed provocatively,
and just behind her the monk Nonnus.
Nonnus taps her on the shoulder.
He is smiling broadly.

NONNUS
Sister Pelagia, I presume.

PELAGIA
(she doesn't know him]
Sister! You must be joking.

NONNUS
Not my sister. God's.

PELAGIA
(bursts out laughing.]

NONNUS
Father Nonnus, at your service.

PELAGIA
Father? Now you've really got me confused!

NONNUS
That's just the beginning.

The psalm singing finishes.
Nonnus hushes Pelagia
as Athanasius rises to preach.

                    ATHANASIUS
                (pauses for effect)
                As I was saying—

The crowd goes wild with delight.
Enormous cheering.

76. EXT. TEMPLE OF KOM OMBO.
EARLY MORNING. VERY QUIET.

Ramir is inspecting his domain.
The whole temple is looking neglected and run down.
Very brief vignettes:

77. INT. INSIDE TEMPLE GRANARY.

The grain store is very nearly empty.
Ramir registers this. Thinks. Shrugs.

78. EXT. TEMPLE. AT REAR WALL.

Ramir looks up at a large marvellous carving
 of the crocodile god Sobek [extant].
It is half broken. Ramir ponders briefly.

79. EXT. TEMPLE. AT REAR WALL.

Ramir is looking closely at the medical frescoes
[extant]. Small smile.

80. EXT. TEMPLE AREA. CROCODILE TRAP.

*Ramir is looking down from above
at one fairly large crocodile caught in the trap.
A stone pit. Not much water.
The gate from the trap to the river is closed.
Crocodile is very lethargic.
It has been there for a very long time.*

81. INT. GOVERNOR'S OFFICE.
LATE MORNING.

*Governor Flavius is seated.
Ramir in High Priest's garb stands before him.
The exchange is icily polite, but deeply bitter on both
sides. Governor has the whip-hand and is enjoying it.*

GOVERNOR
I gather you have again
ignored my instructions.

RAMIR
I will continue to measure the Nile
at the solstice and inform you of the result.

GOVERNOR
That's what I thought you'd say.
Well, it's the last time. All measurement of
the Nile will in future be under the direct
jurisdiction of the regional government.
No other announcement of water levels
will be official. Or tolerated.

RAMIR
May I assume that the preferential tax
treatment of the temple will continue.

GOVERNOR
I see no reason why it should. *(pause)*
I will shortly be issuing an edict
concerning the temple school.
In future no such school will be authorised.
All education in this region will be under
the control of the State authorities and of
his Holiness, the Bishop of Kom Ombo.
I refer you to the recent edict by Patriarch
Athanasius concerning the church school
to be attached to the new basilica.
Is that clear?

RAMIR
Perfectly. Whoever controls the youth
controls the future.
But I am glad to know that Athanasius
has been reinstated. Again. *(pause)*
What of the medical and welfare services
of the temple?
Are you going to transfer those too?

GOVERNOR
You are permitted to continue them.
But no state subsidy will be available
to provide staff or provisions.

RAMIR
There are reports of outrageous and
murderous attacks upon temples in other
regions. By organised armies of monks.
I am sure Patriarch Athanasius has not
authorised such fanatics. Can I be assured
of military protection if any such events
occur here?

GOVERNOR *(brief anger)*
Athanasius would not be Patriarch again
were it not for the outrageous murder of
George the Cappadocian— But let that pass.
As you know, our garrison is considerably
stretched, now that conflict with the Nubians
has unfortunately flared up again. So I regret
I can offer you no guarantees. But we will,
of course, do our best to protect any innocent
citizens.

RAMIR
(finally almost losing his cool)
Since you clearly intend to remove both the
tax exemption and payment for the temple
school, since you have already transfered the
gold depository, and now the granaries, to the
city council, since you refuse to guarantee our
very safety in the event of an armed attack,
how do you expect the temple to survive?

GOVERNOR
Frankly, I don't.
Imperial policy at present is tolerant.
And for the moment you have the
peculiar protection of Athanasius.
But I don't expect your temple
to outlast this generation.
Nobody believes in you any more.
The cross has conquered.

RAMIR
On this basis, our finances will not last
another six months, let alone a generation.
What do you expect me to do?
I can't simply walk away.

                    GOVERNOR
Why not? *(sarcastic relish)* Of course,
if you need a flow of ready cash, there's a
growing market for disused cult statues.
The Emperor has even started a trend
recently, shipping some old obelisks to
Constantinople. Do you have any spare
obelisks? And you could probably find
a few wealthy purchasers for your
magnificent frescoes. Rich people always
like walls covered with pretty pictures.

                    RAMIR *(under control again, icy)*
Thank you for your suggestions.

Ramir turns on his heel and walks out.
Governor smirks complacently.

82. EXT. TEMPLE. THE LARGE HYPOSTYLE
HALL. DAY.

Ramir is addressing assembled workers and temple
staff. About ten are left. Including Panib.
They are despondent.

Ramir is standing before a large incised
and painted wall fresco of the hawk god Horus,
as in the opening pan shot.

He is strangely exhilarated but keeping it in check.

                    RAMIR
All I can offer you now is three months work.
Those who want to apply for employment on
the new basilica, or the governor's public
buildings, are of course free to do so.

He pauses. Workers look at each other.
But nobody makes a move to leave.

                    WORKER-2
            We could finish some of those repairs,
            at least.

Murmurs of agreement. Ramir waits.

                    RAMIR
            I have something rather different in mind.
            (pause)
            It would take about three months.
            And it would require all your old skills.
            But in a new way.

They are intrigued. Ramir pauses.
Then continues. Quietly. Firmly.
Measured rhetoric:

                    RAMIR
            The Governor and the christians want
            this temple to rot, to crumble into decay.
            They will raid it for building materials,
            and for what they call 'pretty pictures'.
            They will inscribe their slogans.
            They will deface our gods. *(pause)*
            We will not let them. *(pause)*
            Our gods have served us well.
            They have looked after us in this world.
            They have promised we could live for ever,
            in a better world.
            But this is not a better world.
            This is not a world in which our gods
            would want to live for ever. *(pause)*

Our gods no longer need to live in this world.
Their images no longer delight in our daily
ritual, but await only insult and desecration.
They do not need to be looked at
by those who do not believe in them.
They do not wish to be looked at
by those who mock them.
Mock them, yet still fear them. *(pause)*
The christians know there is power in our
gods, in our temple, in this house of god.
That is why they will seek to destroy it.
(pause)
We will not let them. *(pause)*
We will take that power from them.
The cross will not conquer.
It will have nothing to conquer.
Victory will not be theirs.
Only a fear that remains.
After our gods have gone.
Of their own accord. At our hands.
The hands of those
who love and respect them.
(Ramir holds out his hand to Panib)
Please.

Panib finally gets the point.
He hands his mallet and chisel to Ramir.

Ramir turns to the fresco behind him
and begins to chisel very carefully
at the face of Horus. Obliterating it.

Workers gasp.

Camera moves in close on Ramir's hands. Holds.

*Then pans slowly from the frescoes
onto the white clothes of Ramir's back.*

*Fade to full white.
(As in the opening pre-credits shot.)*

*SFX: Ramir's hammer and chisel is
gradually joined by sound of
more mallets and chisels.*

83.(SFX OF HAMMER AND CHISEL
continue as the following visuals merge:]

A SEQUENCE OF SHOTS SHOWING
SKILFUL HACKING AT SPECIFIC DETAILS
OF GODS ON THE TEMPLE FRESCOES —
INTERCUT WITH AND MERGED ONTO
OR UNDER LAP-DISSOLVE SEQUENCE OF
VERY BRIEF BUT VIVID SCENES—
ALMOST NIGHTMARE BUT REAL:-

84. EXT. NIGHT. FULL MOONLIGHT.

*Disciplined and fanatical monks in large numbers
attacking and burning a small Egyptian temple.*

Destruction, fire, smoke, murder.

*The monks are dressed identically.
Similar to Pachomius monks, but now with swords
and javelins instead of wooden staffs.*

They are chanting:

" SAINT GEORGE! SAINT GEORGE! "

85. INT. PUBLIC BATHS. NIGHT. FLAMES.

An aged Theon is looking on in sorrow and horror
as piles of manuscripts are burned
as fuel in the furnaces of a public baths.

86. INT. TEMPLE OF SERAPION. NIGHT.

Huge wooden idol (Serapis) is attacked
by a drunken mob of christians.
As someone splits open the idol with an axe,
hordes of mice rush out from it
and run through the mob.

87. EXT. NIGHT.

Hypatia, now grown up, is flayed alive
by a mob shouting:

> "The Cross has conquered"
> "Victory is ours!"

Her mangled body is trampled on.

88. INT. PAN ACROSS TEMPLE FRESCOES,
NOW SKILFULLY DEFACED.

Fade out all sound FX.

Final fade from frescoes, back to full white.

It is now white sunlight.

89. EXT. TEMPLE. SUNLIGHT.
TOWARDS SUNSET.

Ramir, Panib, Shefru, and Kador
are sitting in the shade from the bright setting sun.
Rest of the temple is deserted,
looking much as it does today.

They are eating a simple evening meal and talking.
Relaxed air.
Looking across at the Nile in the near distance.
And towards the sunset.

They are silent until:

                    PANIB
          Our last day.

                    RAMIR
          A few loose ends.

                    SHEFRU
          What do you still have to do?

                    RAMIR
          (has been thinking about this one)
          The crocodile.

                    PANIB
          Ah yes. Young Sobek himself, eh.

                    SHEFRU
          You're going to release it? *(thinks he should)*

                    KADOR *(thinks he shouldn't)*
          Let that ravenous thing back into the river!

RAMIR *(pause)*
I haven't decided.

PANIB
Better to kill it.

RAMIR
(changing the topic— to Kador :)
You're also leaving tomorrow?

KADOR
Yes.

SHEFRU
Aren't you scared?

KADOR
The worst the Romans can do to me
is kill me. Or the mines.
I've survived the mines once.

PANIB
It's a high price.

KADOR
One day, we'll overthrow them.
Chase them out. The empire's already
crumbling. Here they need access to the sea.
They need the routes across the desert.
They need the corn of Egypt.
We can still attack them where it hurts.

SHEFRU
We will think of you.
(slight laugh) In our peaceful oasis.

PANIB
If we ever find it!

KADOR *(teasing)*
Believe your ancestors!
If they say there is a garden
at the beginning of the Nile, trust them!

PANIB
I don't trust any of my family,
however ancient! *(more serious :)*
It may be a very long journey.
And the garden may be a myth.
But I do want to know, finally, where all this
incredible flow of water comes from.
The great Nile, ever-flowing. Look at it!

Looking at the Nile, they fall silent.

A peaceful silence between friends.

Hold for a while— then:

RAMIR *(quietly to Panib)*
One question I wanted to ask you, Panib.
I was told this is a trick known to all builders.

Ramir draws a Pythagoras triangle on the ground.

RAMIR
Is it so? That 3, 4, and 5 give a perfect angle?

PANIB
(considers briefly) Of course.
But we do it an easier way.

Panib reaches into his sack of tools.
He brings out a wooden set-square. Flourishes it.

PANIB
Use one of these!

(General laughter.)

SHEFRU *(teasing)*
So, brother, is that what you're planning?
To teach mathemathics
in the governor's new school!

RAMIR
No, sister, I am still going into the desert,
as I said.
But I keep thinking about numbers.
How big can they get?

KADOR
As big as you like.
So long as they're not Roman soldiers!

PANIB
Any number you can think of,
you can always add another one to it.

RAMIR
(points to the Pythagoras triangle in the sand)
What if I added the numbers
of these three sides together.

PANIB
Easy. 3, 4 and 5. Makes 12.

RAMIR
Twelve what? I can treat any side, any length,
as a unit. To measure with.
So I can call that side a 1.
Then what is the sum of the three sides?
Or I can call that other side a 1 instead.
What then? Not 12 any more.
The sums would be different in each case.

SHEFRU
One what? Decide on your measure,
little brother, before you add them.
There's no mystery.
The angle would still be the same.

PANIB
Like measuring taxes by the Nile!
Did you really not know that one?
We had to maintain the sluice for them!

(General laughter.)

RAMIR
(persists, prepared to be teased)
But what if I added up *all* the numbers?
The total of all possible numbers.
Would that be a number? *(pause)*
And could I still add another 1 to it?
Or would I have discovered a different kind
of number? Not just infinitely large.
Different.

KADOR
(joke and pun) The Great One!

(General laughter.)

SHEFRU
Brother, I hate to think of you sitting in the
hot desert sun thinking about huge numbers!

PANIB
Yes, Ramir, what are you really going to do
in the desert? You can hardly become a—
monk!

(General laughter.)

RAMIR *(pause)*
I think I'll make up a new religion.

General silence. Longish pause.

KADOR
You can't make up a new religion!

RAMIR
Well, no more than I can make up
a new number. *(pause)*
But perhaps I can find one.
A desert religion. Simple.
Awesome. Beautiful. Demanding.
(almost talking to himself)
Just one god. A different god.
Not fighting over images of different gods.
Or different images of the same god.
Beyond all images.

Pause.

Quiet silence.

SHEFRU *(gently)*
We will think of you, brother. *(pause)*
Now, we have a long journey to begin.
Tomorrow.
And we must go and fetch our son.
No school for him tomorrow.

But they do not move. The sun is setting.

They sit watching it as the scene fades.

90. EXT. RIVER NILE. EARLY MORNING.

High aerial shots of boat on Nile.
Echo of opening shots.
But the boat is now heading further south. Full sail.

Quite rapid sequence: sound of wind only.

Boat pulls into a deserted stretch of the east bank,
some miles south of Kom Ombo.
Kador disembarks. Waves briefly.
Sets off into the eastern desert.
He carries the sword he captured.

Boat continues south.
Four figures now visible on board:
Ramir, Panib, Shefru, son Khem (now about 15).

Boat pulls into the west bank. Desert.
Ramir embraces the three on board, disembarks.
Small bag on his back. Plain gellabiah.

He walks firmly into the desert, without looking back.

91. EXT. NILE. SUNLIGHT

*Aerial shots continue on the boat,
heading slowly south with its small family on board.
Over a sequence of extended shots
of the boat on the Nile :*

Written or Voice-Over:]

                AFTER TWO MORE EXILES,
                SAINT ATHANASIUS DIED IN 373 C.E.
                STILL PATRIARCH OF ALEXANDRIA.
                HE HAD OUTLIVED SIXTEEN EMPERORS.
                THE CREED ATTRIBUTED TO ATHANASIUS
                IS STILL RECITED IN
                SOME CHRISTIAN CHURCHES TODAY

                *

                HYPATIA, THE DAUGHTER OF
                THEON THE LIBRARIAN,
                BECAME A RENOWNED PHILOSOPHER
                AND MATHEMATICIAN.
                SHE WAS MURDERED
                BY A CHRISTIAN MOB IN 415 C.E.
                THEY SKINNED HER ALIVE.

                *

                A NEW RELIGION FINALLY
                CAME OUT OF THE DESERT
                AND CONQUERED ROMAN EGYPT.

                IT IS SOMETIMES SAID THAT
                WHEN THE NEW CALIPH WAS ASKED
                ABOUT THE BOOKS STILL IN THE
                GREAT LIBRARY OF ALEXANDRIA,
                HE REPLIED:
                "IF THEY AGREE WITH THE PROPHET,
                WE DO NOT NEED THEM.

IF THEY DO NOT AGREE WITH THE
PROPHET, WE DO NOT WANT THEM."
SO THE FEW REMAINING BOOKS
WERE BURNED.
IT IS ALSO SAID THAT THIS STORY
IS FALSE.

*

IN 1947 C.E. A BURIED JAR
WAS FOUND AT NAG HAMMADI,
NEAR THE ANCIENT MONASTERY OF
PACHOMIUS.
IT CONTAINED TWELVE SCROLLS
OF PREVIOUSLY UNKNOWN TEXTS,
HIDDEN AROUND 350 C.E.

*

NONNUS THE PRIEST
CONVERTED THE COURTESAN PELAGIA.
HE BECAME A BISHOP.
SHE BECAME A SAINT.

*

GEORGE THE CAPPADOCIAN
IS TODAY REMEMBERED
AS "SAINT GEORGE"
FIGHTING HIS DRAGON :
ATHANASIUS

WE DO NOT KNOW WHAT HAPPENED
TO THE LAST PRIEST OF HORUS.
—OR TO THE CROCODILE

92. EXT. CROCODILE TRAP.

The crocodile is still there.
The gate to the river is open.
But the crocodile does not move. It may be dead.

93. EXT. RIVER NILE. SUNLIGHT. NO BOAT.

Written or Voice-Over:]

        BUT CROCODILES NO LONGER LIVE
        NEAR THE TEMPLE OF KOM OMBO.

FINAL CREDITS OVER:]

94. EXT. KOM OMBO TEMPLE WALL.
HORUS FRESCOES.

*Fade from Nile river shots to a long very slow
tracking shot across the greyish defaced wall
of Kom Ombo temple—as it is now.*

                    END